UPROOTING THE RURAL POOR IN RWANDA

Human Rights Watch
New York · Washington · London · Brussels

Copyright © May 2001 by Human Rights Watch
All rights reserved.
Printed in the United States of America.

ISBN:1-56432-261-0
Library of Congress Card number: 2001090057

Cover photo:Shelters in Rwandan imidugudu.
© Human Rights Watch
Cover design by Rafael Jiménez

Addresses for Human Rights Watch
350 Fifth Avenue, 34th Floor, New York, NY 10118-3299
Tel: (212) 290-4700, Fax: (212) 736-1300, E-mail: hrwnyc@hrw.org

1630 Connecticut Avenue, N.W., Suite 500, Washington, DC 20009
Tel: (202) 612-4321, Fax: (202) 612-4333, E-mail: hrwdc@hrw.org

33 Islington High Street, N1 9LH London, UK
Tel: (171) 713-1995, Fax: (171) 713-1800, E-mail: hrwatchuk@gn.apc.org

15 Rue Van Campenhout, 1000 Brussels, Belgium
Tel: (2) 732-2009, Fax: (2) 732-0471, E-mail:hrwatcheu@skynet.be

Web Site Address: http://www.hrw.org

Listserv address: To subscribe to the list, send an e-mail message to majordomo@igc.apc.org with "subscribe hrw-news" in the body of the message (leave the subject line blank).

Human Rights Watch is dedicated to
protecting the human rights of people around the world.

We stand with victims and activists to prevent
discrimination, to uphold political freedom, to protect people from inhumane
conduct in wartime, and to bring offenders to justice.

We investigate and expose
human rights violations and hold abusers accountable.

We challenge governments and those who hold power to end abusive practices
and respect international human rights law.

We enlist the public and the international
community to support the cause of human rights for all.

HUMAN RIGHTS WATCH

Human Rights Watch conducts regular, systematic investigations of human rights abuses in some seventy countries around the world. Our reputation for timely, reliable disclosures has made us an essential source of information for those concerned with human rights. We address the human rights practices of governments of all political stripes, of all geopolitical alignments, and of all ethnic and religious persuasions. Human Rights Watch defends freedom of thought and expression, due process and equal protection of the law, and a vigorous civil society; we document and denounce murders, disappearances, torture, arbitrary imprisonment, discrimination, and other abuses of internationally recognized human rights. Our goal is to hold governments accountable if they transgress the rights of their people.

Human Rights Watch began in 1978 with the founding of its Europe and Central Asia division (then known as Helsinki Watch). Today, it also includes divisions covering Africa, the Americas, Asia, and the Middle East. In addition, it includes three thematic divisions on arms, children's rights, and women's rights. It maintains offices in New York, Washington, Los Angeles, London, Brussels, Moscow, Dushanbe, and Bangkok. Human Rights Watch is an independent, nongovernmental organization, supported by contributions from private individuals and foundations worldwide. It accepts no government funds, directly or indirectly.

The staff includes Kenneth Roth, executive director; Michele Alexander, development director; Reed Brody, advocacy director; Carroll Bogert, communications director; Barbara Guglielmo, finance director; Jeri Laber special advisor; Lotte Leicht, Brussels office director; Michael McClintock, deputy program director; Patrick Minges, publications director; Maria Pignataro Nielsen, human resources director; Jemera Rone, counsel; Malcolm Smart, program director; Wilder Tayler, general counsel; and Joanna Weschler, United Nations representative. Jonathan Fanton is the chair of the board. Robert L. Bernstein is the founding chair.

The regional directors of Human Rights Watch are Peter Takirambudde, Africa; José Miguel Vivanco, Americas; Sidney Jones, Asia; Holly Cartner, Europe and Central Asia; and Hanny Megally, Middle East and North Africa. The thematic division directors are Joost R. Hiltermann, arms; Lois Whitman, children's; and Regan Ralph, women's.

The members of the board of directors are Jonathan Fanton, chair; Lisa Anderson, Robert L. Bernstein, David M. Brown, William Carmichael, Dorothy Cullman, Gina Despres, Irene Diamond, Adrian W. DeWind, Fiona Druckenmiller, Edith Everett, Michael E. Gellert, Vartan Gregorian, Alice H. Henkin, James F. Hoge, Stephen L. Kass, Marina Pinto Kaufman, Bruce Klatsky, Joanne Leedom-Ackerman, Josh Mailman, Yolanda T. Moses, Samuel K. Murumba, Andrew Nathan, Jane Olson, Peter Osnos, Kathleen Peratis, Bruce Rabb, Sigrid Rausing, Orville Schell, Sid Sheinberg, Gary G. Sick, Malcolm Smith, Domna Stanton, John J. Studzinski, and Maya Wiley. Robert L. Bernstein is the founding chair of Human Rights Watch.

ACKNOWLEDGEMENTS

This report was researched and written by staff of the Africa division of Human Rights Watch. Michael McClintock edited the report, which was also reviewed by James Ross, Rachel Reilly, and Joanne Csete. Human Rights Watch thanks William Seltzer and Herbert Spirer for assistance in assessing statistical information.

Tamar Satnet and Patrick Minges provided production assistance.

Human Rights Watch gratefully acknowledges the support of NOVIB for this work.

TABLE OF CONTENTS

I. SUMMARY 1

II. RECOMMENDATIONS 4
    To the Rwandan government: 4
    To U.N. agencies and nongovernmental organizations: 4
    To donor governments: 5

III. BACKGROUND 6
    Historic Patterns of Settlement 6
    Population Growth and Land Scarcity 6
    Property and Returning Refugees 7
    The Housing Crisis 8

IV. THE NATIONAL HABITAT POLICY 11

V. IMPLEMENTATION 14
    The East: Kibungo, Umutara, and Kigali-Rural 15
    The Northwest: Ruhengeri and Gisenyi 17
    Elsewhere in Rwanda 17

VI. POPULAR REACTION TO IMIDUGUDU 19

VII. FILLING THE IMIDUGUDU: THE USE OF COERCION 23
    Obeying the "Law" 23
    The Security Argument 24
    Avoiding the Move 26

VIII. THE USE OF FORCE 28
    Kinigi Commune 29
    Resisting Relocation 30
    Dissent by Local Officials 31

IX. FORCED DESTRUCTION OF HOUSES 34

X. LAND 39
    The Link to Imidugudu 39
    Landholding Laws and Practices 40
    Taking the Land 42
    Land for the Imidugudu 42
    "General Sharing Scheme" 45
    "Returning" Property 45
    Land Taken for Large-Scale Farms 50
    Remedies for the Dispossessed 52
    Effect of Land Loss on Cultivators 54

    Opposition to Loss of Land 55

XI. WOMEN, CHILDREN, AND THE ELDERLY 57

XII. RECONCILIATION 61

XIII. NUMBERS 65
    Returnees from the First Wave of Refugees, 1959-1973 65
    Imidugudu Residents 66

XIV. VIOLATIONS OF HUMAN RIGHTS 68
    Right to Freedom of Movement and Choice of Residence 68
    Right to Adequate Housing 70
    Right to Secure Enjoyment of One's Home 72
    Right to Freedom of Opinion and of Expression 72
    Right to Property 72
    Right to Remedy 73

XV. THE ROLE OF THE INTERNATIONAL COMMUNITY 74
    Donors 74
    U.N. Agencies 79
    Nongovernmental Organizations 83

XVI. DIALOGUE WITH THE RWANDAN GOVERNMENT 85

XVII. CONCLUSION 91

I. SUMMARY

The Rwandan government has resettled hundreds of thousands of Tutsi refugees who came home after decades of exile, four years of war, and the 1994 genocide that killed at least half a million Tutsi living inside Rwanda. This report deals not with that resettlement, which has drawn general praise, but rather with another, less well-known process which took place in its shadow and which resulted in violations of the rights of tens of thousands of Rwandan citizens.

On December 13, 1996, the Rwandan Cabinet adopted a National Habitat Policy dictating that all Rwandans living in scattered homesteads throughout the country were to reside instead in government-created "villages" called *imidugudu* (singular, *umudugudu*). Established without any form of popular consultation or act of parliament, this policy decreed a drastic change in the way of life of approximately 94 percent of the population. In the subsequent four years, the Rwandan government moved hundreds of thousands of citizens into imidugudu, a significant number of them against their will.

The government adopted the habitat policy to achieve long-term development goals enunciated by the dominant Rwandan Patriotic Front (RPF) years before, but it then linked this rural resettlement plan to efforts to end the housing crisis provoked by the return of the refugees. As international agencies and donor governments hurried to assist in housing the returnees, the government ordered that all new houses be built within government-designated settlements. Hundreds of thousands of homeless Rwandans, most of them Tutsi returnees, but some of them survivors of the genocide and other victims of the conflict, moved willingly to the settlements.

At the same time and without fanfare, local authorities began insisting that rural-dwellers who had homes, both Tutsi and Hutu, move to imidugudu. It even compelled home-owners to destroy their houses before making the move. High-level national officials claimed to have never authorized coercion to enforce this policy, but they knew that local officials used threats and force to make people move. They praised communes where residents moved most quickly to the settlements and even promoted the prefect of Kibungo, the region where the policy was implemented most rigorously.

Officials carried out rural reorganization first in the east where returnees were most numerous and where the control of property threatened to become a major source of conflict. Later, after suppressing an insurgency in the northwest, soldiers and local authorities enforced the habitat policy there, asserting that regrouping people into imidugudu was essential to their security.

In several cases, Rwandans who spoke openly against the policy of forced resettlement or who refused to obey the order to destroy their homes and move to imidugudu were punished by fines or arrest.

The first to relocate, many of them Tutsi returnees or genocide survivors, received ready-built homes or materials for construction from foreign-funded agencies. Those who moved later, many of them Hutu or Tutsi who were obliged to leave solid homes, received little or no assistance. Many of them lacked the resources to build houses and cobbled together temporary shelters of wood, grass or leaves, and pieces of plastic. Some have lived in such temporary shelters for two years or longer. According to information gathered in late

1999 by the United Nations Development Program and the Rwandan government, well over half a million imidugudu residents live in such shelters or in unfinished houses.

Many of those who have suffered most from forced villagization are women and children who are heads of households.

In implementing the rural resettlement program, local officials in many communities established imidugudu on land confiscated from cultivators, most of whom received no compensation. The choice of the site was often made without popular consultation.

In conjunction with establishing imidugudu, local officials provided land to repatriated Tutsi refugees who had none. In parts of Kibungo, Umutara, and Kigali-rural prefectures, they obliged landholders to share their holdings with those who came from outside the country. Officials made this decision, too, without popular consultation. Those who were compelled to divide their property ordinarily received no compensation for the part lost. Some of those who refused to cede part of their property to others were punished by imprisonment. Authorities also appropriated land for officials, military officers, and their associates, including businessmen, and permitted these powerful persons to confiscate land for themselves. The recipients are supposed to develop large-scale farms to benefit the local and national economy.

In imposing and implementing the National Habitat Policy, the Rwandan government violated the rights of tens of thousands of its citizens:

- by compelling them to reside other than where they choose
- by arbitrarily and unlawfully interfering with their homes
- by obliging them to destroy or cede their property without due process and without compensation.
- by punishing those who spoke out against this policy and
- by failing to provide adequate remedy for those whose rights were violated.

When the policy was first implemented, the international community was still coming to terms with its sense of guilt for having done nothing to halt the genocide. Eager to atone by funding shelter for the homeless, donors, U.N. agencies, and international nongovernmental organizations (NGOs) poured tens of millions of dollars and substantial human resources into construction programs. Even as they did so, most of them knew that the housing programs were intertwined with a rural resettlement program that had occasioned multiple human rights abuses. At first they discussed these problems, but they then lapsed into silence before the determined Rwandan effort to carry the policy through. Only after two—or in some cases three—years did most donors again begin to question the lack of popular participation in the program and other abuses that it entailed.

Whether in response to international criticism, shortage of funds, or domestic opposition, the Rwandan government slowed implementation of the policy during the year 2000. But it did not alter its determination to move all rural-dwellers eventually to imidugudu and it was obliging people in the southwestern prefecture of Cyangugu to move to the settlements as the year ended.

This report is based upon field work in ten of the twelve prefectures of Rwanda (Butare, Byumba, Cyangugu, Gisenyi, Gitarama, Kibungo, Kigali, Kigali-rural, Ruhengeri, and Umutara) as well as on interviews with officials of the Rwandan government, staff of

Summary

embassies in Kigali, and representatives of various international agencies and nongovernmental organizations. It draws also on documents from the Rwandan government, the United Nations, and diplomatic sources.

II. RECOMMENDATIONS

To the Rwandan government:

1. Order all civilian and military authorities to cease immediately any use of force, intimidation, or threat to compel rural-dwellers to leave their homes against their will to reside in imidugudu. Investigate charges against government officials accused of violating this order and impose legally-provided administrative sanctions if they have done so.

2. Initiate a widespread public information campaign to inform all citizens that they are not required to move to imidugudu and will suffer no consequences for deciding to remain in their homes.

3. Permit those now in imidugudu to return to their homes if they so desire and provide those who destroyed their homes on government order with reasonable assistance in rebuilding them. Assure that needed resources are provided to the most vulnerable persons, including particularly women and children.

4. Ensure that those who ceded land for imidugudu receive compensation for the property ceded and have access to a legal remedy if they are dissatisfied.

5. Permit free discussion of national policies on housing, land, and economic development.

6. Make no further large grants of land to persons or associations until the National Transitional Assembly establishes a policy and a legal basis for such cessions.

7. Ensure that future decisions on housing and land issues not lead to violations of human rights protected by Rwandan law and international convention.

To U.N. agencies and nongovernmental organizations:

8. Review all available information to ascertain whether your support contributed, willingly or unwillingly, to the violation of the rights of rural-dwellers forced from their homes. If this was the case, adopt procedures to prevent this from happening in the future. Lobby donor governments to bring pressure on the Rwandan government to halt the forcible displacement of rural-dwellers and to remedy past violations.

Recommendations

To donor governments:

9. Refuse to provide any financial, technical, or other support for Rwandan government projects that involve the forcible displacement of people from their homes and lands and the destruction without reasonable compensation of homes and other property.

10. Offer assistance to the Rwandan government in assessing and improving the current policies and practices on land and housing, with particular attention to the rights to choice of residence, to adequate housing, and to the secure enjoyment of one's home.

III. BACKGROUND

Historic Patterns of Settlement

For centuries Rwandans have lived in homesteads scattered on the hills, their houses set inside enclosures which are surrounded by cultivated fields. In addition to growing crops, most farmers raised small livestock such as goats, chickens, and rabbits. Wealthier farmers possessed one or a small number of cattle. The dispersed habitat permitted intensive cultivation with farmers using household waste and animal manure to fertilize their fields. Living next to their fields also allowed farmers to protect their crops from thieves, a safeguard that recently has become especially important: some 70 percent of Rwandans are now below the internationally-recognized poverty line and many are hungry enough to steal food.[1] Rwandans favored living surrounded by their land not just for the practical advantages but also because they valued privacy highly.

Although Rwanda had a highly organized state for centuries, it had no cities before the twentieth century. The ruler frequently moved his court from one region to another so there was no political locus for urbanization. Markets, although held regularly at the same locations, never grew into substantial permanent settlements. After a colonial administration was established in the early 1900s, the capital, Kigali, and several prefectural towns developed around administrative centers, but both then and after independence, authorities discouraged movement to urban centers.

The colonial administration established some rural settlements called *paysannats* to encourage the growth of cash crops. They were largely unsuccessful. After independence, the Rwandan government created other paysannats, some to accommodate Tutsi displaced in ethnic violence and others to provide fields for land-hungry people from the northwest. Officials were apparently beginning to see benefits in changing patterns of settlement, but they launched no large scale effort to reorganize rural life.

Population Growth and Land Scarcity

In the years following independence, the Rwandan population grew rapidly, reaching an annual growth rate of 3.1 percent a year in the period 1980-1990 and making Rwanda at that time the most densely populated country in Africa.[2] At first agricultural production kept pace with population growth, but in the 1980s poor growing conditions and decreasing fertility of the soil reduced returns to farmers. Growing numbers found it impossible to accumulate cash reserves and had to sell land to meet urgent needs, such as medical expenses. By the end of the 1980s landholdings were increasingly unequally divided: those

---

[1] Government of Rwanda, Ministry of Lands, Human Resettlement and Environmental Protection, "Thematic Consultation on Resettlement, Background Paper," July 2000, p. 6, quoting the World Bank, *Rwanda Poverty Update*. Hereafter cited as Government of Rwanda, "Thematic Consultation."

[2] Republique Rwandaise, Ministère du Plan, Service National de Recensement, *Recensement général de la population et de l'habitat au 15 août 1991. Enquête postcensitaire*. Kigali, 1993.

who had access to extra-agricultural resources (chiefly salaried work) obtained control over a growing proportion of agricultural land while those who relied exclusively on farming held a shrinking part.[3] Increasing numbers of young men faced the prospect of receiving no land at all in a culture where land was needed in order to legitimately marry and establish a household.

The fall in agricultural productivity and the increase in numbers of landless or virtually landless cultivators had enormous significance in a society where more than 90 percent of the population lived from farming. Usually unable to find jobs outside agriculture, the landless rented or borrowed land, worked as laborers in the fields of others, or remained unemployed.

Property and Returning Refugees

In 1993 the Hutu-led Rwandan government and the Tutsi-led RPF, which had been at war for nearly four years, signed the Arusha Accords, a peace agreement which among other provisions guaranteed refugees the right to return to Rwanda. Most refugees were Tutsi and the children of Tutsi who had fled Rwanda after the 1959 revolution which ended Tutsi rule. Providing land for the returnees, expected to number in the hundreds of thousands, was a major issue, given the already dense rural population throughout Rwanda. The parties recognized that the returnees had rights to the property which they had left in the country. But in the interests of "social harmony and national reconciliation," they "recommended" that returnees not claim property which had been left more than ten years before and subsequently occupied by others, the case for the holdings of most Tutsi refugees.

The parties agreed to provide returnees instead with land and materials to build homes in settlements which would include health centers, schools, roads, and access to water.[4] According to one observer at the negotiations, RPF delegates were adamant that the new homes must be built in "villages." They asserted that rural poverty in Rwanda resulted from the pattern of dispersed homesteads and that villages were necessary to serve as magnets to promote economic development.[5]

The accords failed to bring peace. When combat resumed in April 1994, an interim Rwandan government launched a genocide that killed at least half a million Tutsi and many Hutu opposed to the authorities and the genocide.

---

[3]Catherine André, "Terre Rwandaise, Accès, Politique et Réforme Foncières," in F. Reyntjens and S. Marysse, eds., *L'Afrique des Grands Lacs, Annuaire 1997-1998* (Paris: Harmattan, 1998), note 20, p. 150 and pp. 158-9.

[4]Protocole d'Accord Entre le Gouvernement de la République Rwandaise et le Front Patriotique Rwandais sur le Repatriement des Réfugiés Rwandais et la Reinstallation des Personnes Déplacées, June 9, 1993, articles 3, 4, 13, and 28. Hereafter cited as Protocole d'Accord.

[5]Human Rights Watch interview, Washington, by telephone, January 12, 2001.

The growing poverty and land scarcity fueled the genocide and help to explain the readiness with which the jobless and the landless took to killing Tutsi, whether for immediate payment or in return for the promise of land.[6]

When the RPF defeated the interim government, hundreds of thousands of Tutsi refugees returned from exile.[7] At the same time, some two million Hutu fled the country at the order of the defeated government. Many of these new refugees took flight also because they heard reports—some true, some false—of massacres and summary executions of civilians by RPF soldiers.[8]

After the RPF established its government in July, 1994, there was no immediate housing crisis because most new arrivals settled in the homes of those who had fled or who had been killed. Nonetheless the Rwandan government soon began drawing up plans for the kind of settlements stipulated in the accords, locating them on previously unoccupied lands, mostly in a national park and hunting range in eastern Rwanda. Various NGOs, including those funded by the office of the United Nations High Commissioner of Refugees (UNHCR), began construction soon after.[9] Several NGOs also rebuilt damaged houses and constructed new ones in scattered locations rather than in settlement sites.[10]

The Housing Crisis

In 1995 and 1996, the Rwandan government repeatedly requested international action to defuse a growing threat from refugee camps in Zaire (later the Democratic Republic of the Congo, DRC). The defeated government was using the camps as a base from which to reorganize and rearm its soldiers and Interahamwe, the militia responsible for much of the killing during the genocide. When there was no response from the international community, the Rwandan government sent its troops across the border. Together with local allies, they attacked the refugee camps, killing tens of thousands of civilians as well as thousands of combatants. They also sent hundreds of thousands of Rwandans back to Rwanda, thousands of them against their will, and they chased tens of thousands of refugees further west into the forests of Zaire. At the same time, Tanzania pushed Rwandans there to repatriate. In the space of a few weeks, nearly 1.3 million refugees returned to Rwanda.

---

[6]In the early days of the genocide, government officials began redistributing property vacated by victims, sometimes to local leaders of the killing. Human Rights Watch/Alison Des Forges, *Leave None to Tell the Story: Genocide in Rwanda* (New York, Human Rights Watch and the International Federation of Human Rights Leagues, 1999), pp. 299-300.

[7]The figure usually cited is 800,000 Tutsi returnees. See below.

[8]Human Rights Watch/Des Forges, *Leave None to Tell the Story,* pp. 702-723.

[9]Juvénal Nkusi, "Problématique du Régime foncier au Rwanda. Contexte et perspectives, relations avec l'habitat regroupé," Conseil de Concertation des Organisations d'Appui aux Initiatives de Base, May 2000, pp. 26-27.

[10]Draft working paper, Anonymous, "Imidugudu, Assessment of Housing and Land Reform Plans in Rwanda," May 1997, p. 7. Hereafter, Anonymous, "Imidugudu."

Background

Rwandan authorities had assured Hutu returnees that they could reclaim their homes and lands. They had formalized the guarantee in a ministerial order in September 1996 which spelled out the procedure for repossessing property and set a fifteen day deadline for returning property to those who reclaimed it.[11]

When the Hutu returned suddenly and in massive numbers beginning in November 1996, some of them succeeded in reclaiming their property, thus displacing Tutsi who then needed other homes. In many other cases, Hutu failed to get their homes back and they also needed shelter. In addition, some survivors of the genocide had seen their homes destroyed. Although they possessed property and perhaps even a building, some preferred not to return to their places of origin and were seeking homes elsewhere. Similarly Hutu victims of war sought help, although they were more likely to want to restore their original homes than to want to establish themselves elsewhere.

The housing crisis was real, but it may have been less serious than it was presented at the time. In early 1997, the Ministry of Planning estimated that 254,000 households required assistance with housing.[12] The Ministry of Rehabilitation and Social Reintegration came up with the similar figure of 250,000 families, or some 1,270,000 people.[13] This amounts to more than one and a half times the number of Tutsi returnees, estimated then at 775,000.[14] This estimate itself may be exaggerated, as discussed below, but even if it were accurate, not all 775,000 returnees needed housing; significant numbers, including the thousands who took over property in the city of Kigali, were able to continue occupying homes vacated by previous owners who were dead or who did not return. In addition, not all the needy required new homes. Thousands of damaged houses were available that could be inhabited after being repaired.

The sense of crisis was heightened by the concentration of needy persons in the eastern part of the country where they clustered in numbers far greater than could be served by locally available housing resources. More Tutsi returnees settled in Kibungo and Umutara, the prefectures nearest the border crossings where they entered from Uganda and Tanzania, than anywhere else in Rwanda. In addition, this flatter, eastern part of Rwanda offered good pasturage for cattle and was traditionally favored by Tutsi over hillier regions to the west.

---

[11]Republic of Rwanda, Ministerial Order No. 01/96 of September 23, 1996 Regarding the Temporary Management of Land Property.

[12]Omar Bakhet, UNDP Resident Representative and U.N. Resident Coordinator, Memo to Ambassadors, Charge d'Affaires and Heads of UN Agencies, January 23, 1997. The number of persons is based on an estimated five persons per household as established in Republic of Rwanda and United Nations Population Fund, *Socio-Demographic Survey 1996, Final Report,* (Kigali, January 1998), p. 41.

[13]Anonymous, "Imidugudu," p. 9.

[14]Rwanda and United Nations Population Fund, *Socio-Demographic Survey 1996,* p. 30.

In late 1996, returnees who had been born abroad constituted 42 percent of the residents of Umutara and 19 percent of those in Kibungo.[15]

Kigali-rural also experienced greater pressure for property than other prefectures to the west or south. Although only about 5 percent of its residents were born abroad, it included an additional 15 percent who had been born in other prefectures of Rwanda, a consequence of the drawing power of the national capital which lay at its heart.[16]

---

[15]Republic of Rwanda and United Nations Population Fund, *Socio-Democraphic Survey 1996*, pp. 28-29. The actual percentage of returnees would have been even higher because these numbers do not account for refugees who had been born in Rwanda.

[16]Ibid.

IV. THE NATIONAL HABITAT POLICY

When the Cabinet met on December 13, 1996, RPF representatives decided to push ahead with the program of re-organizing rural life that they had espoused since the time of the Arusha negotiations. Over the strong objections of some ministers, they adopted a National Habitat Policy requiring all rural-dwellers to change their way of living. By this time, the vast influx of refugees had begun, but as the text of the decision shows, the ministers adopted the policy to deal with long-range issues of land distribution and economic development, not to resolve the immediate housing crisis of the returnees.

The introduction to the document focuses on issues of population growth and urban migration in the "Third World" and only once, at the end, briefly mentions the "tragic events" of war and genocide as circumstances aggravating housing problems in the Rwandan case. The return of the refugees is referred to only once fleetingly in the twenty-two page document to explain the need to deal with issues of habitat. The Arusha Accords, later cited by authorities erroneously as the legal basis for requiring Rwandans to live in settlements, is not mentioned at all.

The text cites economic development as the reason for imidugudu and says they will serve the following functions:

- to create non-agricultural employment and so reduce pressure on the land;
- to regroup residents to counter the dispersion which makes it difficult to "persuade" them [to follow government policy] (*rend difficile la sensibilisation de la population*);
- to resolve the problem of land scarcity by redistributing the land and creating terracing;
- to protect the environment;
- to improve the transportation and distribution networks.[17]

The policy seems to have been designed for gradual implementation. The text proposes, for example, that authorities establish markets and services at the sites before trying to attract residents to them. Even with such attractions, the text remarked, people would not move "spontaneously" and might need considerable time before being persuaded to accept a new system of settlement and land tenure. The text also foresees the need to compensate persons whose land was taken to serve as settlement sites.[18]

Three weeks after the December 13 decision, Rwandan authorities linked the new habitat policy to efforts to deal with the housing crisis provoked by the return of the refugees. On January 2, 1997, the minister of the interior and communal development required all Rwandans to provide "mutual assistance" to the homeless in constructing new houses. The order focused largely on organizing this assistance through the long-established practice of obligatory labor for the public good, known as *umuganda*. But the minister also

---

[17]République Rwandaise, Ministère des Travaux Publics, Politique Nationale de l'Habitat, December 1996, p. 20.

[18]Ibid., pp. 17, 21-22.

used this directive to explicitly prohibit landowners from building homes on their own holdings if these were outside imidugudu. He said rural-dwellers "...should live apart from the fields."After enumerating several of the groups that would be henceforth living in imidugudu, he wrote, ". . . in brief, everyone is required to take a lot [for housing] in the settlement."[19]

On January 9, 1997 the minister of public works ordered that all Rwandans would receive land to build houses in the imidugudu and that it was henceforth forbidden to build any house outside such a site. He directed local authorities to promptly list all existing houses in their areas to ensure that no new ones were built outside the settlement site. He concluded by making all relevant authorities responsible for "mobilizing people to comply with the policy."[20]

By these two orders, authorities grafted the National Habitat Policy onto programs for housing the homeless. They went beyond the Arusha Accords, which had agreed to provide housing in settlements but which had not excluded returnees from making their own arrangements to build homes elsewhere.[21] Authorities now prohibited such construction—and not just by returnees, but by any Rwandan.

Just as insisting that all new houses be built in the settlements offered a way to hasten rural reorganization, so drawing on international assistance for housing provided resources needed for implementing the habitat policy. Apparently to make it easier to exploit this opportunity, government officials began describing the establishment of imidugudu more as a response to the housing crisis than as a longer-range program to improve land use and stimulate economic development. In a presentation to foreign donors at the end of January 1997, Minister of Rehabilitation and Social Integration Patrick Mazimhaka claimed that imidugudu would promote peace and reconciliation and that they would provide security.[22] These supposed objectives, missing from the December 13 text and apparently first unveiled at this time, coincided perfectly with the rationale of "prevention [of further conflict]" and "protection" used by UNHCR to justify supporting the housing construction program.[23]

---

[19]Republic of Rwanda, Instruction du Ministre de l'Intérieur et du Dévéloppement Communal No. 001/97 du 2/1/1997 Relative à l'Entraide Mutuelle, article 4 (a), *Journal Officiel de la République Rwandaise,* p. 3 Hereafter cited as Republic of Rwanda, Instruction. . . Relative à l'Entraide Mutuelle.

[20]Instruction Provisoire No. MINITRAPE 01/97 sur l'Habitat, articles 11, 15, and 19, *Journal Officiel de la République Rwandaise,* p. 6.

[21]Protocole d'Accord, articles 3, 4, 13, and 28.

[22]Anonymous, "Imidugudu," p. 4.

[23]Chantal Laurent and Christian Bugnion, "External Evaluation of the UNHCR Shelter Program in Rwanda 1994-1999," UNHCR, Reintegration and Local Settlement Section, 2000, pp. ix-xi, 29.

UNHCR was the most important channel of funds to housing programs throughout the whole period.

V. IMPLEMENTATION

The Rwandan state is highly centralized and intensively administered. Local officials are accustomed to passing on policies decided at the national level to the people of their districts. Speaking of the habitat policy, one local official said, "The national government gave the rules. We report back on the progress...."[24] Prefects supervised implementation in their prefectures, but often left such decisions as the location of the imidugudu to the administrative heads of communes, known as burgomasters, who were supposed to be advised by a committee which was composed exclusively of government officials.[25] Councilors *(conseillers)*, who head sectors within the commune, and cell leaders *(responsables)*, who head the cells that make up the sectors, carried out the policy at the grass roots level.

All these officials delivered instructions to the population during "persuasion" meetings, sessions meant both to inform local residents about the new policy and to convince them of its benefits. They said that the new sites would be provided with services, such as water supply, schools, markets, and easy access to roads. They stressed that people living together would be more secure and would find it easier to develop the local economy.

According to a written policy statement from the Ministry of Interior and Communal Development in 1997, resettlement was to be voluntary.[26] And in February 1997, Christine Umutoni, Director of Cabinet at the Ministry of Rehabilitation and Social Integration, stated that "no one will be forced to go along with a program of villagization," although she did admit that "it may be discouraged to stay behind."[27] Regardless of these pronouncements in Kigali, local authorities made clear to citizens out on the hills that they had no choice but to follow the policy and would be subject to fines or other punishment if they did not cooperate.[28]

As is usual with nationally-directed campaigns in Rwanda, the prime minister and other ministers, as well as their immediate subordinates, visited different parts of the country

---

[24]Human Rights Watch interview, Cyimbogo, Cyangugu, May 16, 2000.

[25]One of the seven members was the councilor from the sector concerned. When the committee was set up, councilors, like other committee members, were government appointees, but in March 1999 councilors were elected.

[26]Dorothea Hilhorst and Mathijs van Leeuwen, "Villagisation in Rwanda," Wageningen Disaster Studies, no. 2, 1999, Rural Development Sociology Group, Wageningen University, The Netherlands, p. 16.

[27]Minutes, Meeting of diplomats regarding housing policies of the Rwandan Government, February 12, 1997, p. 3. Hereafter cited as Minutes, Meeting of diplomats regarding housing policies, February 12, 1997. Minutes provided by one of several diplomatic representatives in attendance.

[28]Human Rights Watch, field notes, Cyeru commune, Ruhengeri, July 1999; see below for other examples.

Implementation   15

to lend their authority to the campaign. More recently, President Paul Kagame too went to the hills to praise successful cases of resettlement. The national radio broadcast announcements promoting imidugudu and pressing people to cooperate with the program.[29]

The December 13 text gave no deadline for executing the policy, but once implementation began, some officials stated that all Rwandans were to move to imidugudu within five years and, in some regions, the deadline was set for two years.[30]

The East: Kibungo, Umutara, and Kigali-Rural

Although rural life was to be reorganized everywhere, officials began the effort first and carried it through most rigorously in the eastern and south-eastern prefectures of Kibungo, Umutara, Kigali-rural. It is understandable that authorities acted first in the region with the greatest need for housing, but they clearly meant to push forward rural reorganization as much as to provide new homes. In some cases, local officials even halted on-going housing repair programs that could have provided housing relatively rapidly and cheaply. According to the Ministry of Planning in early 1997, some 84,000 damaged houses nation-wide could have been made habitable by repairs.[31] Making repairs was much faster than building anew and, according to housing experts, cost only one quarter to one third as much. But repairing houses, most of which were located outside imidugudu sites, would have enabled residents to continue living in dispersed homesteads in violation of the habitat policy. So officials ordered CARE-UK and several agencies funded by U.S. assistance as well as UNHCR to halt repair programs and to direct their efforts to the slower and more costly process of building houses in imidugudu. A housing rehabilitation program at Murambi, Umutara, funded by the German government also encountered official opposition, although it is unclear if the work there was actually halted. Similarly authorities discouraged NGOs from continuing to build new homes in scattered locations.[32]

Authorities hastened the implementation of the habitat policy as much to control land as to provide housing. As they regrouped the population rapidly, they also took land for

---

[29] Radio Rwanda news program, May 18, 1999, at 8 p.m., reported a visit by the prime minister and other dignitaries to the northwest; on February 17, 2000 it reported a similar visit by officials to Kibuye. Short features, like one heard on national radio at 7:30 a.m. on December 27, 1999, advertised the benefits of life in imidugudu. See also "Life Has Returned Everywhere in Ruhengeri Prefecture," *Imvaho,* no. 1272, February 22-28, 1999.

[30] Anonymous, "Imidugudu," p. 1; Hilhorst and van Leeuwen, "Villagisation in Rwanda," p. 34.

[31] Omar Bakhet, UNDP Resident Representative and U.N. Resident Coordinator, Memo to Ambassadors, Charge d'Affaires and Heads of U.N. Agencies, January 23, 1997.

[32] Human Rights Watch interview, by telephone, Washington, September 14, 2000; Anonymous, "Imidugudu," pp. 5, 7, 8, note, p. 27; Hilhorst and van Leeuwen, "Villagisation in Rwanda," pp. 34, 37; Minutes, Meeting of diplomats regarding housing policies of the Rwandan Government, February 21, 1997, p. 2. Hereafter cited as Minutes, Meeting of diplomats regarding housing policies, February 21, 1997.

redistribution to Tutsi returnees or permitted them to take land for themselves. Officials also appropriated land to constitute larger holdings for private exploitation, as discussed below.[33]

By February 1997, only weeks after the ministerial orders on habitat were issued and as international agencies were scrambling to build homes for the needy, authorities began ordering local residents to abandon their existing homes for temporary shelters in imidugudu.[34]

Even more than his counterparts in the other two prefectures, the prefect of Kibungo undertook to move all residents—Tutsi or Hutu, homeowner or homeless—rapidly into imidugudu. National officials praised his implementation of the habitat policy and eventually promoted him to head the more important prefecture of the city of Kigali.[35] One year after the campaign began, the prefectural office issued a statement saying that "No policy in Kibungo features [as] so important as villagisation. Kibungo is at the heart of the national villagisation campaign."[36]

Pressured to relocate everyone by the end of 1998, local officials in Kibungo hurried the construction programs. In one area, people were given only one week to move to the designated site.[37] As Rwandans previously resident in their own homes were forced into imidugudu, the demand for housing far exceeded the capacity of the various agencies, which in any case focused largely on building houses for homeless Tutsi returnees and genocide survivors. Local authorities permitted ever shoddier houses to be built. As the resouces which had paid salaried workers were exhausted, the new residents—many of them Hutu—received no help and were told to build their own houses. Many lacked the time and resources to build solid, mud-brick homes and they settled instead for wood-and-mud daub structures.[38] The weakest and poorest of the new residents could manage to build only fragile shelters of wood, leaves, and pieces of plastic. Rwandans call such a make-shift shelter a *blindé,* from the French word meaning tank or armored personnel carrier. The term, which ironically contrasts the fragility of the shelter to the solidity of a military vehicle, apparently refers to the shape of the shelter—something like a small hangar—or to the blue plastic sheeting sometimes used to cover it. Some Rwandans first saw the sheeting used to cover

---

[33]Republic of Rwanda and United Nations Population Fund, *Socio-Demographic Survey 1996*, pp. 28-29; Juvénal Nkusi, "Problématique du Régime foncier," pp. 26-27; Human Rights Watch interview, by telephone, Washington, September 14, 2000.

[34]Minutes, Meeting of diplomats regading housing policies, February 12, 1997; Minutes, Meeting of diplomats regarding housing policies, February 21, 1997; and European Community Humanitarian Office-Rwanda, Note for the File, Shelter funding criteria, February 5, 1997.

[35]Hilhorst and van Leeuwen, "Villagisation in Rwanda," p. 37.

[36]Ibid., p. 37.

[37]Ibid., p. 42.

[38]Ibid., p. 34.

military tanks of U.N. peacekeeping troops which arrived in Rwanda in 1994. Some residents of imidugudu have inhabited blindés for two years or more.

The Northwest: Ruhengeri and Gisenyi

Officials expected the northwestern prefectures of Ruhengeri and Gisenyi to be among the last where the habitat policy would be implemented. Largely Hutu in population, this area constituted the power base of the former regime. It was suspected of continuing hostility to the RPF-run government and its residents were thought likely to resist the order to move to settlements.[39] Relatively few Tutsi returnees had settled there so the need for housing and land was limited and it seemed unlikely that the powerful would seek to establish large landholdings in the area.

The situation changed during 1997 and 1998 as insurgents, known as *abacengezi*, led a serious uprising against the government. Using bases in the DRC, they took control of some parts of the northwest and raided into central Rwanda. In the course of suppressing the insurgency, soldiers and officials displaced more than 650,000 people into camps, more to keep them from supporting the insurgents than to protect them from attack. By mid-1998, the government forces were largely in control of the area and officials were preparing to disband the camps. Authorities saw this as an "opportunity" to hasten the creation of imidugudu and ordered the displaced to move to newly designated settlement sites rather than return to their own homes.[40]

Officials had started citing security needs as a reason for imidugudu in early 1997 and they referred to them frequently, often in situations where no actual threat existed (see below). In the northwest, however, they had real concerns for security and apparently saw establishing imidugudu as one way to reduce the likelihood of any recurrence of the insurgency. An official document of November 1998 stressed that resettlement in imidugudu would be a "key factor" in assuring security as well as development.[41]

The process continued throughout 1999 and early 2000 as more and more people of the northwest, including those who had not been displaced in the conflict, were obliged to move into imidugudu.

Elsewhere in Rwanda

In other prefectures local officials carried out the habitat policy in a more relaxed fashion. With fewer returnees in these areas, they had both less demand for housing and, often, fewer resources available to build settlements. They may also have anticipated—and in some cases actually encountered—substantial resistance to imidugudu in parts of central

---

[39] Anonymous, "Imidugudu," p. 10.

[40] Republic of Rwanda, Ministry of Gender, Family and Social Affairs, "Guidelines on the Settlement of IDPS in Northwest," November, 1998, pp. 1.

[41] Ibid., pp. 1-2.

Rwanda.[42] Authorities in these other prefectures, such as Byumba and Gitarama, sometimes permitted the construction of houses outside imidugudu or, at least, the repair of existing structures.[43]

During 2000 officials delayed rural reorganization in some areas, including the northwest. In some communities residents who had been told to prepare to move before the next growing season were allowed to remain in their homes and cultivate as usual. In others, settlement sites were laid out but construction was postponed. In the southwestern prefecture of Cyangugu, however, officials in such communes as Cyimbogo and Gisuma continued moving people into imidugudu, reportedly pressing to meet a deadline of the end of the year.[44]

Variations in speed and strictness aside, the overall success in moving large numbers of people to imidugudu was remarkable. By the end of 1999, three years after the policy was announced, some 90 percent of the population of Kibungo and some 60 percent of the population of Umutara resided in the new settlements.[45] In Ruhengeri, virtually all the people from half the communes as well as many others had been resettled at the new sites.[46]

Information gathered by the United Nations Development Program (UNDP) together with Rwandan government officials in late 1999 suggests that some 1,080,000 or approximately 14 percent of Rwandans have moved to imidugudu.[47] Even if somewhat exaggerated by official sources, this figure still represents an extraordinary restructuring of rural life in a very short time. For many the move to imidugudu was voluntary and presumably to their advantage, but for tens of thousands of others, the move was made under coercion and apparently to their detriment.

---

[42] Anonymous, "Imidugudu," p. 10; Minutes, Meeting of diplomats regarding housing policies,, February 12, 1997, pp. 2-3 Human Rights Watch interview, Kigali, May 23, 2000.

[43] Human Rights Watch interview, by telephone, Washington, September 14, 2000.

[44] Human Rights Watch interview, Kigali, October 23, 2000.

[45] Human Rights Watch interview with the Minister of Lands, Human Resettlement, and Environment, Kigali, December 18, 1999.

[46] Human Rights Watch interview, Prefect of Ruhengeri, Ruhengeri, February 25, 2000.

[47] Nations Unies. Programme des Nations Unies pour le Développement (PNUD), *Rapport d'Etude sur les Sites de Reinstallation au Rwanda*, September-November 1999, pp. 6-8. Hereafter cited as PNUD, *Rapport*. See below for further discussion of statistics.

VI. POPULAR REACTION TO IMIDUGUDU

It is impossible to know how many Rwandans favored the habitat policy when it was established because there was no open debate or public participation in making the decision. Incomplete data indicate that attitudes towards the policy varied according to a number of circumstances. A Dutch NGO found that more than 50 percent of a group of genocide survivors in Cyangugu, the prefecture abutting the Congolese border, favored moving to imidugudu; most were widows apparently concerned with security. But the same agency found that only 7 percent of a sample group in the central prefecture of Gitarama were willing to leave their homes and move to imidugudu.[48] A Rwandan government poll in the northwestern prefectures of Gisenyi and Ruhengeri in 1998 found that 41 percent wanted to remain in their own homes and not move to imidugudu.[49] Special representative for Rwanda of the U.N. Commission on Human Rights Michel Moussalli sampled opinions of residents in three imidugudu in 1999: in two settlements, residents expressed no complaints, but in the third a significant number said they had been moved against their will.[50]

One poll of people now residing in imidugudu found that 74 percent generally favored the settlements, although many immediately qualified this response by mentioning changes that they believed were needed to make life in the imidugudu satisfactory. When asked whether they had gained or lost by the move, 55 percent of the same sample stated that they had lost—economically, in terms of quality of life, or in other ways.[51]

Whatever the exact range of opinion, it is clear that a significant minority of rural-dwellers in some places and a majority in others did not or do not want to live in the settlement sites.[52] According to the current policy, they have no choice and if they do not now live in the settlements, they will sooner or later have to move there.

Some who are dissatisfied protest the way the policy was imposed by national officials without consulting those most affected by it. One person remarked:

---

[48] Anonymous, "Imidugudu," pp. 15, 24.

[49] United Nations. Economic and Social Council. Commission on Human Rights. "Report on the situation of human rights in Rwanda submitted by the Special Representative, Mr. Michel Moussalli, pursuant to Commission resolution 1999/20," E/CN.4/2000/41, February 25, 2000, p. 32. It is not specified if all the remaining 59 percent favored a move or if they expressed other views.

[50] Ibid, pp. 32-33.

[51] Association Rwandaise pour la Défense des Droits de la Personne et des Libertés Publiques (ADL), *Etude sur la Situation des Droits Humains dans les Villages Imidugudu* (Kigali, 2000), pp. 37, 42. Hereafter cited as ADL, *Etude*.

[52] In addition to data presented below, see Hilhorst and van Leeuwen, "Villagisation in Rwanda,"pp. 35, 43 and Rwandan Initiative for Sustainable Development (RISD), "Land Use and Villagisation in Rwanda," September 1999, paragraph 3.3.1. Hereafter cited as RISD, "Land Use."

People don't see the advantages of the imidugudu although there have been a lot of "persuasion" meetings with local and higher government authorities. It is being imposed on us. We have nothing to say. It has been decided, that's it. . . .

The authorities did an opinion poll [in the northwest], so they know people don't want this, especially with no means to build new homes. . . . They say there are many problems here: not enough schools, poverty, sickness. Now they are creating yet another problem. Now we will settle in plastic sheeting. . . . After all these meetings, I don't know if I'll ever really understand why they made this policy. We have a tradition of living apart, having our own space. To move to imidugudu, we find that harassment.[53]

Others are most concerned about the economic losses connected with the relocation. Homeowners or renters who had improved their previous residences lost their investment when they abandoned these homes to move to imidugudu. Those who took mortgages to build or improve their houses are supposed to continue paying their debt although they are no longer permitted to reside in the houses. At the same time the large number of persons who received little or no assistance must find money or materials for the new construction. Some had to pay officials in order to receive what they consider to be a desirable place in the umudugudu. Some had to give up all or part of their fields to serve as sites for the new housing.[54]

Most residents still live primarily if not solely from the produce of their fields and worry about getting to their land, maintaining its fertility, and protecting the crops. One study concluded that imidugudu residents now must travel about 2 kilometers or over one mile further to reach their fields than when they lived in their previous homes. The time and energy needed to travel the additional distance each day must be subtracted from the resources that the cultivator can devote to his or her work.[55] Cultivators say that the greater distance from home to fields makes it impractical to continue the well-established practice of using household waste to fertilize the land. They worry too that being distant from their fields makes it impossible to protect the crops against animals or thieves who could come at night to steal the harvest. One poor woman widowed during the genocide said, "My field is the land where my parents lived, about thirty minutes away from here. Thieves now steal the crops I planted there."[56]

---

[53]Human Rights Watch interview, Ruhengeri, December 3, 1999.

[54]Human Rights Watch interviews, Karago, Gisenyi, October 30, 1999; RISD, "Land Use," paragraph 3.2.3.1. For the issue of land appropriated for housing sites, see below.

[55]ADL, *Etude*, p. 32.

[56]Human Rights Watch interview, Muhazi, Kibungo, November 30, 1999; also interviews at Nkumba commune, Ruhengeri, November 18, 1999; Mutura commune, Gisenyi, November 22, 1999; Umutara, March 16, 2000; Bicumbi, Kigali-rural, March 17,

Many who lived from the land also raised livestock at their old homes, at least chickens and rabbits, if not the more valuable goats, sheep, pigs or cattle. Because imidugudu allot such small parcels of land, many now find it impossible to keep farm animals.[57] One man from Cyangugu explained that in his previous residence, he and his family owned some small livestock which formed their reserve to deal with unexpected needs, such as repairing the house. This they no longer have.[58]

Some residents have expressed worries about hygiene and disease. Many imidugudu lack latrines, clean water, and health facilities.[59] According to UNDP studies, the country-wide average distance from home to clean water is 1.2 kilometers while residents in some imidugudu in Byumba and Cyangugu must walk between 20 and 25 kilometers to find water. Similarly, the national average distance from home to health facility is 4.6 kilometers, but residents in some imidugudu must travel more than 8 kilometers for the most basic health assistance and more than 20 kilometers to a health center.[60] With people living in such close proximity, diseases can spread rapidly. In one umudugudu in Cyangugu, twenty-seven people fell seriously ill the same day and all had to be hospitalized.[61] One man who now lives in an umudugudu situated in a dry, barren stretch of the southeast commented, "Life in the umudugudu is all right, except for the sun, hunger, and sickness."[62]

Many who did not initially oppose the habitat policy have since become dissatisfied with the way it has been implemented. Officials promised that imidugudu residents would have greater access to basic services and would be well-placed to benefit from new efforts at economic development. Such has not been the case for most. According to a study by UNDP, 81 percent of the sites still lacked water in late 1999.[63] Another study concluded that among the imidugudu residents sampled, the average person must travel some four kilometers or nearly two and a half miles further to reach fields, school, water and source of firewood than when he or she lived in his or her previous home.[64]

One resident of Bicumbi commune, Kigali-rural prefecture, expressed his discontent:

2000; and Cyimbogo, Cyangugu, May 16, 2000.

[57] ADL, *Etude*, p. 37.

[58] Human Rights Watch interview, Cyimbogo, Cyangugu, May 16, 2000.

[59] Human Rights Watch interviews, Rutonde, Kibungo, April 15, 1999.

[60] Common Country Assessment, Working Paper no. 3, Resettlement and Reintegration, January 2000, p. 12. (Hereafter cited as CCA Working Paper.)

[61] Human Rights Watch interview, Cyimbogo, Cyangugu, May 16, 2000.

[62] Human Rights Watch interview, Nyarubuye, Kibungo, June 23, 2000.

[63] PNUD, *Rapport*, p. 18; Human Rights Watch interviews, Nyamugali, Ruhengeri, November 18, 1999.

[64] ADL, *Etude,* p. 32.

We have been here [in the umudugudu] for seven months. . . . But for my family, the situation is not good. Our field is very far. The cows [belonging to others] come and ruin our crops. We have no water. They said that life in the umudugudu would be extraordinary—with water, school, electricity, a good road! But here we are under plastic sheeting. They promised houses but I see nothing. You find me under this sheeting with holes in it that the rain comes through.[65]

In August 1999 the Catholic bishops wrote the Rwandan president to protest against the use of force in moving people to the sites, but this criticism was not made public.[66] Although the press occasionally published information about individuals who have suffered from the policy, it rarely aired more general opposition. When rural-dwellers spoke against forced movement to imidugudu in their own communities, they were sometimes punished, as described below. In an exceptional case in August 2000, people in Kibungo profited from the rare visit of President Kagame to their area to complain about the habitat policy. Their comments were heard on national radio, perhaps encouraging further criticism. In October, the radio broadcast a meeting during which one person took to task members of the national commission on unity and reconciliation and the national human rights commission. He remarked that people in Kibungo were forced to leave comfortable homes and to go live under plastic sheeting in imidugudu and asked if these national human rights defenders found this "normal," meaning acceptable. A commission member replied that they had no legal powers to halt abuses and could act only by denouncing abuses. He did not explain why the commission had not yet publicly denounced abuses related to rural reorganization.[67]

Small numbers of insurgents who appeared again in the northwest in 2000 tried in one case to increase popular resentment and fear of the imidugudu. When they attacked in Rwerere commune, Gisenyi prefecture, in May 2000, they launched a mortar at an umudugudu and they left tracts accusing the Rwandan government of regrouping Hutu in "concentration camps" in order to "eliminate" them.[68]

Rather than openly opposing the habitat policy, most Rwandans who found it unjust treated it as one more burden to be endured. "You can't expect us to sleep with an empty stomach and then have the strength to complain," said a Tutsi widow whose husband was slaughtered in 1994. "We need to deal with living in the umudugudu just like we deal with losing members of our family."[69]

---

[65] Human Rights Watch interview, Bicumbi, Kigali-rural, March 17, 2000.

[66] Human Rights Watch interview, Gisenyi, December 8, 1999.

[67] Radio Rwanda, "Kubaza Bitera Kumenya," October 8, 2000.

[68] Human Rights Watch interviews, Gisenyi, June 5, 6, and 7, 2000.

[69] Human Rights Watch interview, Muhazi, Kibungo, November 25, 1999.

VII. FILLING THE IMIDUGUDU: THE USE OF COERCION

When houses were completed in the early phase of the imidugudu program, many of the intended beneficiaries—including Tutsi returnees—declined to occupy them. They refused for different reasons: because promised support services had not been provided, because land for farming or pasturage was not being distributed at the same time, or because they found the property they then occupied more attractive than that offered in the site. The early occupancy rate was so low that it raised questions among donors and implementing agencies about whether housing was really needed and, if it were, why the program was not meeting the need.[70]

Obeying the "Law"

By mid-1997 local officials in Kibungo began pressing people with growing urgency to move to imidugudu. In repeated public meetings and in visits to the homes of the recalcitrant, officials delivered the same message: that people must move.[71] Some officials may have deliberately misstated the situation by saying the new policy was "the law." A man in Kibungo remarked, "It is only the law that says we have to live grouped together."[72] A woman in Umutara expressed the same idea. "It's the law that the whole population has to live in imidugudu." Although she had been in the settlement for two years, she said, "I don't know if I can say we *live* here. That's the way it is—we are here because we must obey the law, that's all."[73] Whether or not officials explicitly stated that the policy was law, the impact of their words was the same. The power of the authorities, *ubutegetsi,* so far surpassed that of the individual that most citizens felt compelled to obey. As one man who had to sacrifice his own home in Bicumbi commune explained, "You know our state, you know its orders. We just execute them. We can't ask why. We just do it."[74]

As one woman widowed during the genocide explained:

The councilor said, "Leave your houses." "It's required," the authorities said.
"Even if you have nowhere to go, even if you must use banana leaves for a
roof, just leave your houses." Then we had to build a blindé in one week's time.
I went to find someone to help, a neighbor, but I had to pay him 3,000
Rwandan francs [about U.S.$7.50]. The house I had to leave was built by an NGO.

---

[70]Anonymous, "Imidugudu," pp. 6, 10, 37; RISD, "Land Use," paragraph 3.3.1.

[71]Human Rights Watch interviews, Rutonde and Muhazi, Kibungo, April 15, 1999; and Cyeru, Ruhengeri, July 3, 1999.

[72]Hilhorst and van Leeuwen, "Villagisation in Rwanda," p. 43.

[73]Human Rights Watch interview, Umutara, March 16, 2000.

[74]Human Rights Watch interview, Bicumbi, Kigali-rural, March 17, 2000; for similar sentiments in Gikongoro, see RISD, "Land Use," paragraph 3.3.1.

It is still there, but thieves came and stole the roof.[75]

Officials combined the carrot and the stick in their efforts to get people to leave their homes. They promised assistance to those who moved promptly and threatened the recalcitrant that they too would have to move and would receive no help, either then or in the meantime. This tactic was especially effective with the weak and vulnerable who knew how difficult it would be to set up a new house alone. A Tutsi woman from Muhazi commune whose husband was killed during the genocide related how she came to move to an umudugudu:

> For us survivors, we were forced. No one refused because we were brought here by force. . . . The old burgomaster held a meeting and he also asked the councilor to "persuade" everyone. They said, "If you refuse, you won't get any assistance, even your neighbors won't help you. You have to move." It was forbidden even for family members [to help someone who had refused to move]. That really scared survivors—we are poor. We have nothing. We have no one to listen to our problems, so we had to move.[76]

Another Tutsi widow, distressed by having to destroy the house which she had labored to rebuild after the genocide, said that she knew of no one who had been imprisoned or fined for refusing to move. She added, "They only terrorized us, that's all."[77]

In some cases, officials hurried people to move without regard for the usual agricultural cycle, exposing them to loss of their crops. One woman said:

> I used to live in a big house surrounded by my fields. I had built that house after the genocide and moved there in 1997. Here I have been in this blindé for a year. I moved because it was required to move to the umudugudu. The burgomaster held a meeting to tell people to move. We were compelled. . . . We had less than one month to move. This happened in October. Normally in October there are beans that are not yet dry. . . .We moved in mid-October.[78]

The Security Argument

Security was a serious concern for officials and citizens alike in many parts of Rwanda during the period when the habitat policy was being implemented. Although providing protection had not been among the first stated objectives of the policy, officials at the

---

[75]Human Rights Watch interview, Muhazi, Kibungo, November 30, 1999.

[76]Human Rights Watch interview, Muhazi, Kibungo, November 25, 1999.

[77]Human Rights Watch interview, Rutonde, Kibungo, March 14, 2000.

[78]Human Rights Watch interview, Muhazi, Kibungo, November 30, 1999.

Filling the Imidugudu

national and local levels soon began claiming that the settlements offered greater safety than did dispersed homesteads. Some persons, particularly the elderly or women living alone, moved to imidugudu because they expected to be safer living there.[79]

Officials sometimes exploited fear of attacks by Interahamwe, the militia responsible for much of the killing during the genocide, to get the reluctant to move to imidugudu.[80] They warned that those who stayed at home should expect no protection in case of attack.

In the southwestern prefecture of Cyangugu, a local official in Cyimbogo commune used such a threat. Asked to explain why virtually everyone in his area had relocated to imidugudu, he said they decided to move after he told them that the authorities would no longer provide either protection or assistance for any who remained in their homes.[81]

A resident from another part of Cyangugu remarked,

> Here they didn't use force like they did in Ruhengeri. Instead they encouraged people to move and told them that the authorities would no longer provide any services for them if they stayed in their old homes. . . . I suppose that is a kind of force, too, though, isn't it?[82]

A man from elsewhere in the same prefecture, who was Hutu, described how people had left the hills for the umudugudu in his sector. He said that Tutsi survivors of the genocide returned to their own lands after the RPF victory in July 1994, even if their homes had been destroyed, and began rebuilding their houses. Then soldiers of the former Rwandan army and Interahamwe began raiding from across the Congolese border, stealing cattle, shooting at houses, and trying to entice local Hutu to go back across the border with them. The witness continued:

> With this growing insecurity, genocide survivors moved near the road and lived together. At first, we were alone because most other Hutu were in Zaire [now the DRC].
> Those who stayed behind were few. The people in the umudugudu said that our staying on the hills could lead to attacks by the Interahamwe, for example, if we harbored them in our houses. So we were supposed to move to the umudugudu to better protect security.
>
> Some didn't go right away—we had good, solid houses. . . . In the meantime, men in uniform whom we recognized came and killed a cousin a few meters from my house.

---

[79]Human Rights Watch interviews, Nkumba commune, Ruhengeri, November 18, 1999; Mutura commune, Gisenyi, November 22, 1999; and Umutara, March 16, 2000; ADL, *Etude*, p. 37.

[80]Human Rights Watch interviews, Nyamugali, Ruhengeri, November 18, 1999.

[81]Human Rights Watch interview, Cyimbogo, Cyangugu, May 16, 2000.

[82]Human Rights Watch interview, Kamembe, Cyangugu, May 17, 2000.

We went to the authorities to complain. They replied, "If you stay there, we can't ensure your safety." So I built a house [in the umudugudu].[83]

Officials also used the argument of security to coerce people into moving from places and at times when no immediate threat existed.[84] An elderly Tutsi widow and genocide survivor from Rutonde commune, Kibungo, returned from a period in the hospital to find that the young people who had been living with her had been put out and that the local authorities had confiscated the keys to her house. She sought out the councilor and asked for the keys back. He told her that if she returned home, she might be suspected of harboring Interahamwe. He also warned that if Interahamwe came to kill her, the authorities would not intervene to save her. When asked if there had been a risk from Interahamwe at that time—March 1999—, she replied no and added "but I think that there was a law saying that all people must move to imidugudu."[85] So she moved.

Avoiding the Move

Although most citizens who were coerced by the authorities eventually gave in, some found ways to appear to comply while making minimal changes in their way of living. Residents in some communes in Ruhengeri and Umutara built houses in imidugudu but continued occupying their original homes. They passed the night in imidugudu, but each morning headed off to spend the day in their homes. One woman explained that she feared official reprisals if she did not at least seem to be living in the umudugudu. She said, "We are afraid to sleep in our own houses."[86]

Some who are wealthy or well-connected avoided having to move by giving gifts to officials or by making use of ties of kinship or friendship. Occasionally survivors of the genocide were able to count on greater tolerance from officials when they refused to move. Others held their ground, but lived with the fear of reprisals for their refusal to sacrifice their homes.[87]

A Tutsi woman widowed during the genocide and who resisted pressure to move said:

They came to force me, but I pleaded with them and explained that I don't have

---

[83]Human Rights Watch interview, Kigali, May 19, 2000.

[84]Researchers found officials in Kanzenze commune, Kigali-rural, using the argument of security to justify the need to move to imidugudu when there was no apparent threat in the area. Hilhorst and van Leeuwen, "Villagisation in Rwanda," p. 45. For a general statement of the security argument, see Nkusi, "Problématique du Régime foncier," p.29.

[85]Human Rights Watch interview, Rutonde, Kibungo, March 14, 2000

[86]Human Rights Watch interviews, Umutara, March 16, 2000 and Ruhengeri, December 7, 1999.

[87]Human Rights Watch interviews, Muhazi, Kibungo, November 30, 1999. Hilhorst and van Leeuwen, "Villagisation in Rwanda," p. 35.

Filling the Imidugudu 27

the strength to build a new house. They didn't accept my plea. I'm waiting for my punishment. . . . Put me in jail or what have you! They said they would destroy my house, so I'm waiting for that. They said, "If you refuse, you are opposing the will of the government." The government says that everyone must move to the umudugudu.[88]

---

[88] Human Rights Watch interview, Muhazi, Kibungo, November 30, 1999.

VIII. THE USE OF FORCE

Authorities in the east and southeast sometimes talked of security needs to convince and coerce rural-dwellers into relocating, but after early 1997 there was virtually no armed opposition in most of Kibungo, Umutara, and Kigali-rural. In the northwest, however, the insurgents were strong and authorities imposed rural reorganization there largely for security reasons and only secondarily to achieve long-term development goals. During 1997 and 1998 Rwandan soldiers and, less frequently, insurgents targeted civilians, killing or injuring tens of thousands of them. Authorities moved 650,000 civilians to camps, often using force to do so. They claimed to be protecting local people from attack, but they aimed also at making it impossible for them to support the insurgents. Rwandan soldiers suppressed the insurgency by the end of 1998 through intensive occupation of the region and the use of overwhelming force. They generally treated persons caught outside the camps without authorisation as enemies, subject to be shot on sight.[89]

Life in the huge camps was miserable with residents crowded together in inhumane conditions, many of them suffering from malnutrition and exposed to disease. When authorities ordered the move to imidugudu sites in late 1998 and 1999, many residents went willingly because even those sites barren of housing and services at least offered more space than the camps and access to their fields. Soldiers, presumed by many civilians to be hostile to them, ordinarily attended meetings where the orders to move were given and stood ready to enforce them. According to one witness, "Some [of us] were hit and mistreated. We were scared to see the soldiers with their guns, saying that we had to go. So everyone left quickly and we went to the imidugudu."[90]

Most people wanted to go back to their own homes rather than to imidugudu, but they were told that this was not a choice. A resident of Nyamugali commune stated simply, "We were threatened with being shot if we went home."[91] According to one local official in Ruhengeri, "People in my commune who do not want to move to imidugudu are generally considered insurgents."[92] Knowing how quickly soldiers shot anyone thought to be an insurgent, most people moved without question.

---

[89]Reports of the United Nations Human Rights Field Operation and press releases by Human Rights Watch and others documented these killings. See, for example, United Nations, High Commissioner for Human Rights Field Operation in Rwanda, Status reports of March-Mid-May 1997, (HRFOR/UPD/14 March-May 1997/E) and of May-June 1997 (HRFOR/RPT/13 May-June 1997/E).

[90]Human Rights Watch interview, Kinigi, Ruhengeri, December 3, 1999.

[91]Human Rights Watch interview, Kigali, December 10, 1999.

[92]Human Rights Watch interview, Kigali, December 10, 1999.

The Use Of Force

Another Ruhengeri resident said, "No one wanted to go.... The soldiers threatened that anyone who took too long to move would be considered 'accomplices' [of the enemy]. That scared us because we knew the punishment could be death."[93]

Kinigi Commune

The commune of Kinigi abuts the northern border of Rwanda and is subject to frequent incursions. There the authorities moved virtually the entire population into imidugudu between January and August 1999. Many families were obliged to relocate in the span of a few days or weeks. One local resident related, "We were told to come see the lots for the houses on February 22, 1999. By March 1, we had to be in imidugudu—the whole sector."[94] National and prefectural officials praised the speed and thoroughness of the relocation in Kinigi; they delivered a "bravo" to the commune for its "massive response" to the program.[95]

A resident of Kinigi said the move to the umudugudu was accompanied by less violence than what he had witnessed in previous months. He said:

> The soldiers ensured security and enforced the move here because it was the authority of the state, the public authority.... Coming here to the umudugudu was a duty. The army only controlled the move of people towards the site.... In general there was no brutality. Just executing the government orders.[96]

Another Kinigi resident said that local authorities warned they would employ force if needed to implement the policy. "They didn't specify what kind of force," he said. "But we understood what they meant."[97]

In many respects, the situation in this commune exemplified the worst aspects of the forced relocation of rural-dwellers. Many people were grouped in one huge agglomeration, where thousands of miserable blindés were awash in mud and water whenever it rained. These make-shift shelters of wood, grass, leaves, and plastic sheeting offered little protection against the cold, damp weather frequent in this mountainous region. Some people lived in these blindés for more than a year.

In August 2000, during a highly-publicized visit to Kinigi, President Kagame promised to provide roofing materials so that people could build houses. The national television filmed

---

[93] Human Rights Watch interview, Kigali, December 10, 1999.

[94] Human Rights Watch interview, Kinigi, Ruhengeri, December 3, 1999.

[95] Radio Rwanda, News broadcast, January 21, 2000; "Inhabitants of Ruhengeri impatiently await regrouped habitat," *Imvaho Nshya*, No. 1288, June 11-20, 1999.

[96] Human Rights Watch interview, Kinigi, Ruhengeri, December 3, 1999.

[97] Human Rights Watch interview, Ruhengeri, December 3, 1999.

the visit to the site but authorities reportedly prevented it from broadcasting the worst scenes of squalor.[98]

Resisting Relocation

Most of the displaced moved from the camps to the imidugudu without protest, both because they feared the consequences of opposition and because they saw the new sites as potentially more habitable than the camps in which they had suffered for many months.[99] But officials encountered more resistance when they began ordering people who had never been displaced to leave their homes for the imidugudu.

In July 1999, Human Rights Watch researchers witnessed a meeting where the councilor told people who had never left their homes during the entire period of war that they must move to the government-designated sites. The councilor was apologetic at having to deliver the bad news, which residents had anticipated for some time, but his distress did little to mitigate their anger.[100]

A month later, at a meeting in another commune in Ruhengeri, local people spoke out against the forced move to settlements. A witness who was present said:

> Three men, one old and two young, criticized the policy publicly. Soon after they were summoned to the commune where they were arrested and put in the communal lock-up. One was held for a week, one for two weeks, and one for a month.[101]

Some who refused to move to imidugudu were fined and arrested.[102] One resident of Ruhengeri related the case of his neighbor:

> One man stayed behind. He said he couldn't leave his potatoes. They weren't ripe yet. The local authorities punished him with a fine of 21,000 Rwandan francs[103] although he asked to be pardoned. He is very poor. He was fortunate though. He could have been killed.[104]

---

[98]Human Rights Watch interview, Kigali, August 10, 2000; Radio Rwanda, News broadcast, August 8, 2000.

[99]Human Rights Watch interview, Ruhengeri, December 7, 1999.

[100]Human Rights Watch, field notes, Ruhengeri, July 1999.

[101]Human Rights Watch interview, Kigali, December 10, 1999.

[102]Human Rights Watch interviews, Ruhengeri, Gisenyi, and Kigali, December 3 and 7, 1999; March 4 and 7, 2000.

[103]This is approximately $60 or about one quarter of the average Rwandan yearly income.

[104]Human Rights Watch interview, Kigali, December 10, 1999.

A local official from Ruhengeri reported that he had imposed fines of 2,000 Rwandan francs on people in his sector who had refused to move. This sum, the equivalent of about $5, would be enough to pay school fees for two children for a year.[105]

A resident of Ruhengeri said that in his area authorities were prepared to go beyond imposing fines. He said:

> In my sector, a deadline was set at a meeting in late November [1999]. People had a week in which to move. When that date came, nothing had happened and the deadline was extended to mid-December. People were told that if they hadn't moved by then they would be punished, not just with a fine—people had paid fines already but still had not moved. The authorities spoke about "other forms of punishment."

There were more than forty families affected by this.[106]

The families decided to move just before the deadline to avoid the "other forms of punishment." In a similar situation in another commune, a witness commented, "No one stayed behind. They only wanted to."[107]

Two local officials from Ruhengeri identified people unwilling to move to imidugudu as opponents of the government and said they should be punished. One said,

> People are not 100 percent for the imidugudu. Some of them don't want to move. Some will be compelled, they will be moved by force. But this is a minority. . . . There are lots of reasons for their reluctance. Some don't want to support the government. There are insurgents. That's one reason, the main one. Some people don't want to move but if they refuse they will be jailed.[108]

Dissent by Local Officials

The lowest level officials, councilors and heads of cells, are closest to the population with whom they live and work. Many are themselves cultivators, as much attached to their homes and land as others who live in their jurisdictions. Many of them, too, have suffered from the relocation policy.

A councilor in Nyakinama commune, Ruhengeri, was reportedly jailed for opposing the move to the imidugudu. As one person familiar with the case commented, "Anyone who questions this policy is accused of collaborating with the abacengezi."[109]

---

[105] Human Rights Watch interview, Kigali, December 10, 1999.

[106] Human Rights Watch interview, Kigali, December 10, 1999.

[107] Human Rights Watch interview, Ruhengeri, December 3, 1999.

[108] Human Rights Watch interview, Ruhengeri, November 18, 1999.

[109] Human Rights Watch interview, Ruhengeri, December 7, 1999.

According to one resident of Ruhengeri, another councilor was singled out for punishment in August 1999. The witness said,

> The councilor was publicly slapped by the assistant prefect because he did not enforce the villagization policy. When the assistant prefect and the burgomaster visited the sector, they saw that little progress had been made on villagization and that even the councilor himself was still living in his old house. They accused him of not having made an effort to "persuade" people about imidugudu. So they called together people from the whole cell for a meeting near the cell office and the assistant prefect slapped him in the face. The burgomaster and assistant prefect were accompanied by a military officer, a captain, and at least five others. . . . [110]

Rather than openly oppose the policy itself, local officials sometimes sought to lessen its impact on residents. Several councilors in Ruhengeri failed to enforce orders that residents work six days a week at building their houses in imidugudu and permitted them to use three days instead to cultivate their fields. Two of these local officials were jailed in the communal lockup for having shown such leniency.[111]

One official expressed his disappointment at how the policy had been implemented and recounted his efforts to ease the burdens of relocation in his sector:

> If the policy had been well planned, we would at least have been able to reimburse people who lost their fields for a village site. If we provided taps, people would have easier access to water. At first, we thought the imidugudu would be financed by the government, but now we see that we will not receive any assistance. We thought, for example, that we would get metal roofing so that people could do their part and build. We made noise at the prefecture and said that people at least need sheeting to keep rain from entering their shelter. So we wait and we keep complaining, hoping that someone will hear us. . . . At least, for now, there is sun. Starting in September, people will come again to ask us what they can do when rain falls into their shelters. . . .
>
> People here are very attached to their fields. Maybe if we had given them houses, they wouldn't long so much for their fields. But as it is, when they are still under plastic sheeting after many months, they don't see why they can't just transfer the sheeting and put it up in their fields, where their houses used to be.[112]

Another official who had to order people to move delayed the deadline to give them time to harvest their crops. He said, "People will not have enough to eat if they have to

---

[110]Human Rights Watch interview, Kigali, December 10, 1999.

[111]Human Rights Watch interview, Kigali, May, 2000.

[112]Human Rights Watch interview, Gisenyi, June 6, 2000.

harvest and build at the same time." He also looked ahead with concern to the net growing season when people might still be engaged in building and not have enough time to work their fields.[113]

---

[113]Human Rights Watch interview, Nyamugali, Ruhengeri, November 18, 1999.

IX. FORCED DESTRUCTION OF HOUSES

It is ironic that a policy presumed to be addressing a housing crisis resulted in pushing hundreds of thousands of people out of their homes and into inadequate shelters, where some have dwelled for months or even years with no immediate prospect of a permanent home. It is doubly ironic that homeowners in some areas were forced to destroy their own houses before moving to imidugudu where they had to cobble together blindés from the remnants of their former homes, sticks, grass, and pieces of plastic.[114]

One assistant burgomaster from Ruhengeri asserted that after a number of "persuasion" meetings, local people were "completely convinced and applauded" the idea of moving to imidugudu. He said this is why they hurried to dismantle their homes of their own free will.[115] A woman who lived in the same prefecture challenged this idea, saying: "It's the policy. Of course, normally, people would not want to destroy their homes to go live in an umudugudu. This is a big problem, the destruction of houses. People have other work to do besides building new houses!"[116]

Another woman from Kibungo expressed similar sentiments, saying that people in her commune were still angry about having had to dismantle their homes two years ago before moving into imidugudu where many still live in blindés.[117]

People convinced that they would have to leave their homes sought to salvage what they could before departure. Most who had houses with metal roofing tried to salvage the sheets of metal, which represented a considerable investment. Those told to move in the rainy season were especially under pressure to save roofing materials. One man related, "Many houses were already destroyed [during combat]... but others—like mine—were still standing. We needed to dismantle them quickly to have some shelter—it was the rainy season."[118]

According to one woman in Umutara, "Many, many people had to destroy their homes. They knew that they were required to leave and they saw that the houses in the umudugudu were not finished. So they dismantled their old homes to have something to finish the new ones."[119]

In some cases, the effort to salvage roofing was futile because the nail holes could not be well enough repaired to make the roof rain-proof. One poor widow who survived the genocide tried to use pieces of her old roof to cover a new, smaller house in the umudugudu.

---

[114]Since most Rwandan houses are built of mud brick or adobe, removing the roof usually leads to their destruction during the next rainy season.

[115]Human Rights Watch interview, Ruhengeri, November 19, 1999.

[116]Human Rights Watch interview, Ruhengeri, December 3, 1999.

[117]Human Rights Watch interview, Musaza, Kibungo, October 30, 2000.

[118]Human Rights Watch interview, Ruhengeri, December 3, 1999.

[119]Human Rights Watch interview, Umutara, March 16, 2000.

Forced Destruction of Houses

She had to beg her sister to sell some of her land to get the cash needed to pay someone to build the house and install the roof. But the metal was so damaged that the house was uninhabitable. She and her children have gone to live temporarily with a neighbor. Someone from Ibuka, the association of genocide survivors, promised to help build her a more solid house; their workers began but have not finished the job. "I don't know why," she said. "Maybe they think I am too poor to have the right to a house."[120]

Another woman widowed in the genocide described the pressure put on people in her region of Kibungo to dismantle their houses in October 1999. She said:

> At a meeting, the authorities said, "Anyone who refuses, we will come destroy your house." Then they did destroy the house of one man. The cell leader asked the neighbors to come destroy his house. At that time, it was just terrible. He had already started building his house in the umudugudu and he just wanted to finish it before moving. He hadn't finished the roof yet. They said, "No, the deadline has arrived."[121]

In parts of the northwest, a substantial number of homes were destroyed or damaged during the insurgency in 1997 and 1998, many by Rwandan army soldiers, some by insurgents. But even in an area like Nkuli commune, next to the forest and the site of months of fighting, 410 of the 613 families in one sector still had homes when they were compelled to move to imidugudu in October 1999. In some regions, like the northern sectors of Cyeru, virtually all homes were intact in July 1999.[122] Many of the owners of these houses destroyed them when they left for the imidugudu. One witness said, "Our house was not really damaged during the insurgency. But we had to destroy it when we left for the umudugudu. We managed to save the roof and doors, but the rest was looted. We had only two to three days. . . to destroy it and get out."[123]

As with the order to move, the order to dismantle houses was sometimes couched in terms of security needs. Said one lieutenant in the army, "Well, if there was force used, if houses were destroyed, we did it to save the lives of the people."[124]

In some areas officials argued, perhaps with some justification, that insurgents might be able to use vacated structures scattered across the hill. But officials in areas that had not been troubled by the insurgency and where there was no real threat used the same justification. A man who now lives with his family in a shelter of mud, sticks, and plastic

---

[120] Human Rights Watch interview, Rutonde, Kibungo, March 14, 2000.

[121] Human Rights Watch interview, Muhazi, Kibungo, November 30, 1999.

[122] Human Rights Watch field notes, July 3, 1999; interview, Nkuli, Ruhengeri, October 31, 1999.

[123] Human Rights Watch interview, Ruhengeri, December 3, 1999.

[124] Human Rights Watch interview, Gisenyi, June 5, 2000.

sheeting in Bicumbi commune, Kigali-rural, saw no sense in the claim that security needs required the destruction of his home. Speaking of the "persuasion" meetings he remarked,

> They said that we must to go to the umudugudu with the others and destroy our houses so that insurgents can't hide inside. If you destroy them, the authorities said, they will have nowhere to hide. . . .This was in June 1999. There were no more insurgents then. They compelled us to destroy our houses, saying that we would find a nice house in the umudugudu. You who drive along the road, doesn't it scare you to see such an awful place as this?[125]

In Umutara, in Murambi commune where there was neither insurgency nor incursions from the border, local officials reportedly ordered the destruction of the houses and crops of three homeowners who were reluctant to leave, claiming that they would be attacked by "infiltrators" if they remained in their homes. In the same commune, the assistant burgomaster and his subordinates were reported to have ordered residents to destroy the sorghum, manioc, and bananas of another homeowner who had refused to cede his land for use as an umudugudu. Some refused to participate in the destruction, saying they did not want to be like the Interahamwe. Local officials then sent the police to enforce their orders. The homeowner sought to protect his rights by appealing to communal authorities, to various ministers, to the prime minister, to the vice president and to the president. Two years of efforts brought him nothing but the enmity of local officials, apparently the cause of his being twice imprisoned in the local lock-up.[126]

One cultivator who also serves as a local official was indignant about the destruction of houses. He said:

> I stayed in my house with my family during the insurgency, even though others went to the camp at the commune office. My house was not destroyed then, though many of our belongings were stolen. I destroyed the house when I came here to the umudugudu. The idea of destroying homes is the will of the state. It compelled people to move to imidugudu. As it was the word of the government, we had to destroy our homes.[127]

Another man from Ruhengeri prefecture expressed similar anger. He recounted:

> At the end of February 1999, we were told to come to the village, to live together. . . . They [i.e., officials] used their authority. I say authority because they destroyed homes. Those with houses in durable materials [baked or adobe

---

[125]Human Rights Watch interview, Bicumbi, Kigali-rural, March 17, 2000.

[126]"The Government of National Unity Should Deal Justly with Old Kilomba Innocent," *Ubumwe*, No. 73, December 22, 1999, pp. 21-2.

[127]Human Rights Watch interview, Ruhengeri, December 3, 1999.

Forced Destruction of Houses

bricks], we had to destroy them by force. They had meetings called and run by soldiers. The soldiers said that anyone still there after March, still in his home, would be considered an accomplice of the Interahamwe.

So we were all compelled to destroy our homes. Some of us don't even have plastic sheeting! Imagine destroying a home made of brick with a metal roof, then looking for grass to build a new one! I can't even call my house a hut, not even a blindé, because blindés have plastic sheeting for roofs. I had a nice house made of stone, with glass windows. But I have destroyed that house. That is the way it is. We have to obey government orders.[128]

Given the overwhelming poverty among rural-dwellers, many Rwandans living in blindés cannot foresee ever being able to build a new home.[129] One woman moved with her husband and children into temporary quarters and was struggling to find money to build a house for her husband's parents, who had been in a plastic-covered grass-and-stick shelter for two years. She remarked in despair, "I just had to destroy my house. I wonder when I'll be able to build another. I have a family to feed, children to put through school. This is a real problem."[130]

Refusal to destroy a house, like failure to comply with orders to move to the imidugudu, could be interpreted as opposition to the government. One widow explained: "We were to destroy our homes when we left. Otherwise it would be a sign that we didn't accept government orders. In that case, the local authorities would ask others to come destroy it. . . . No one refused. It wasn't an option."[131]

Not surprisingly, some people postponed acting. One man remarked, "Some didn't destroy their houses until the last minute, hoping for some change."[132] In some cases where people delayed too long, soldiers arrived to hurry the process. One witness from Ruhengeri commented: "When you heard shots, when shots were fired in the air, people hurried to destroy their houses. Sometimes soldiers came and destroyed one as an example. Then the rest of the people followed suit."[133]

In inquiring into the use of force to make people to move to imidugudu, the special representative for Rwanda of the U.N. Commission on Human Rights found that "There can be no dispute that often for security considerations, some coercion has occurred." He found also that twenty of 150 families in the commune of Gihinga, Umutara had been forced to

---

[128]Human Rights Watch interview, Kigali, December 10, 1999.

[129]Human Rights Watch interviews, Rutonde and Muhazi, Kibungo, April 15, 1999.

[130]Human Rights Watch interview, Ruhengeri, December 3, 1999.

[131]Human Rights Watch interview, Muhazi, Kibungo, November 30, 1999.

[132]Human Rights Watch interview, Ruhengeri, December 3, 1999.

[133]Human Rights Watch interview, Kigali, November 27, 1999.

destroy their homes and to move to the umudugudu. Gihinga was not an area known for security threats.[134]

Officials ordered the destruction of houses most often in Kibungo and Ruhengeri, somewhat less frequently in Umutara and Kigali-rural. Such abuses have happened still less often in other parts of Rwanda, but they are not unknown in Gisenyi, Cyangugu, and Butare. For example, one woman widowed during the genocide who lived in Ntyazo commune, Butare prefecture, was forced to destroy a house she was just finishing and to move to an umudugudu.[135] Commenting on the extent of the practice in his region, one man in Rusumo commune, Kibungo said, "If a house hasn't been destroyed, it has got to be in an umudugudu."[136]

---

[134]United Nations. Economic and Social Council. Commission on Human Rights. "Report . . . by the Special Representative, Mr. Michel Moussalli," p. 33.

[135]Human Rights Watch interview, Buffalo, N.Y., April 28, 2000.

[136]Human Rights Watch interview, Rusumo, Kibungo, June 23, 2000.

X. LAND

The Link to Imidugudu

When the Cabinet established the habitat policy, it envisioned the redistribution of land as well as the relocation of population.[137] A month after its adoption, Minister of Rehabilitation and Social Integration Patrick Mazimhaka stated that the government intended to create "modern, larger scale agricultural production methods" and that people "pushed off the land" by imidugudu and land reform would find other unspecified kinds of employment.[138] Other officials who talked about imidugudu also linked relocating people to redistributing the land. They acknowledged that some people would be deprived of land and said that they would "take on new, useful professions."[139] Three years after the beginning of the policy, Rwandan authorities again reiterated the importance of imidugudu to overall plans for proposed changes in land tenure: "The grouped settlement type (*imidugudu*), as a fundamental factor for optimal land use in the Rwanda context, is part and parcel of the proposed land law."[140]

The government declared that the imidugudu policy was meant to group all rural-dwellers into "villages," but it sometimes opposed the fastest, cheapest, and simplest path to that end: adding new houses to and in the midst of existing clusters of dwellings. Such a plan would also have taken advantage of infrastructure already established in the vicinity of these clusters. In most cases, the government insisted instead that rural-dwellers had to be displaced from their habitual places of residence and hence from the land which was their heritage.[141]

Seeming to echo the January 1997 ministerial instructions that farmers "should live apart from the fields," one expert on land use, currently a deputy in the assembly, suggested in May 2000 that distancing cultivators from their fields would cut their emotional attachment to the land as part of a family heritage. This, he speculated, would make cultivators more likely to treat land as an economic good valued only in terms of its productive capacity.[142] Such a change would presumably make it easier to implement the reorganization of landholding envisioned by the authorities.

---

[137] République Rwandaise, Ministère des Travaux Publics, Politique Nationale de l'Habitat, December 1996, p. 20.

[138] Anonymous, "Imidugudu," p. 4. See also pp. 9-11.

[139] Minutes, Meeting of diplomats regarding housing policies, February 12, 1997, pp. 2, 4.

[140] Republic of Rwanda, Ministry of Land and Human Resettlement, and Environmental Protection, Position on the Discussion Note, January 11, 2000, p. 2.

[141] Anonymous, "Imidugudu," p. 9.

[142] Republic of Rwanda, Instruction . . . Relative à l'Entraide Mutuelle, article 4 (a), p. 3; Nkusi, "Problématique du Régime foncier," p. 31.

These plans had been sufficiently defined by December 1999 for the minister in charge of land to tell Human Rights Watch researchers that the government planned to replace small-scale landholders—the millions for whom the average land holding is now less than one hectare—by a far smaller number of "capable professional farmers" who would exploit holdings of twenty-five, thirty, or even fifty hectares for cattle-raising and cultivating, particularly cultivating cash crops. He explained that those displaced by the large farms would become agricultural laborers on the land they once owned or find other sources of employment. He said that displaced landholders working on such farms near Kigali were "happy" with their new role as agricultural laborers on land which they once owned.[143] The same policy and expectations about large landholdings to be granted to "professional" farmers were reflected in the draft land document circulated by Rwandan government officials in November 2000.[144]

Landholding Laws and Practices
Problems of land in Rwanda are complicated not just because of the high ratio of people to land but also because of the complex patchwork of laws and customs that govern landholding.[145]

In early times, Rwandans saw land as a natural resource, not as the private property of an individual. Persons had the right to use land that they had cleared or that they had obtained from another; they could pass the right of use to their descendants or grant it to others, either freely or in return for services or goods.[146]

With the expansion of state power after the sixteenth and seventeenth centuries, the *umwami*, or ruler, progressively imposed another set of practices based upon the doctrine that he owned everything within his domain, including land which he granted to his subjects for their use. He and his agents tried to require payments of goods or services in return for the use of the land and they sought to exercise the right to dispose of any vacant land. Both Tutsi and Hutu, pastoralists and cultivators, resisted these measures in a number of

---

[143] Human Rights Watch interview, Kigali, December 18, 1999.

[144] Government of Rwanda, Draft document on land policy, distributed at Landnet meeting, November 2, 2000.

[145] For general descriptions, see Ephrem Gasasira, "Regime Foncier et Droit de la Proprieté, (République Rwandaise, Ministère de la Justice, 1996); William Schabas and Martin Imbleau, *Introduction to Rwandan Law* (Quebec: Les Editions Yvon Blais, 1997); and Christopher Harland, "Introduction to Land Law in Rwanda," (Butare: National University of Rwanda, 1998).

[146] In some cases, those who cleared the forest paid something to hunterers and gatherers whom they found on the land.

regions.[147] After Europeans established their administration around 1900, they backed royal efforts to assert authority over land but even with this support, the umwami never established complete control over landholding in the northwest. Kin groups retained extensive rights over the land they had cleared under a system known as *ubukonde*, which is still recognized by the state for the prefectures of Gisenyi and Ruhengeri.[148]

In 1960 the umwami passed ultimate ownership of the land to the state. After the revolution establishing the republic and independence from colonial rule, the burgomaster, as agent of the state, controlled the distribution of vacant lands within his commune while national authorities decided grants of larger expanses of land, particularly those that extended beyond the limits of a single commune.

Europeans had introduced yet another system, a set of written rules to govern land ceded to or bought by proprietors, most of them foreigners.[149] Subsequently Rwandans began increasingly selling land among themselves, a practice that was supposedly regulated by a decree-law issued in 1976.[150] In an effort to slow the growing fragmentation of land holdings, the law set limits to the minimum size of lots that could be sold and it required registry of sales with government officials, but this law remained largely unenforced.

The first article of the 1976 decree-law stipulated that all land not appropriated according to written law belonged to the state, whether encumbered or not by customary rights and whether occupied or not. In 1979, the Rwandan government adopted a law on the expropriation of property in the public interest.[151] In detailing the steps to be followed for a legitimate expropriation, it specified that compensation must be paid for any land registered under the system of written law and that another plot of land (*terrain de réinstallation*) must be provided in exchange for any appropriated land which was held under customary law. It specified also that regardless of whether the land was registered or

---

[147] The uprising led by Ndungutse in 1912 resisted attempts by agents of the court to assert control over land. See Alison L. Des Forges, "'The Drum is Greater than the Shout:' the 1912 rebellion in northern Rwanda," in Donald Crummey, ed., *Banditry, Rebellion and Social Protest in Africa* (Portsmouth: Heinemann, 1986).

[148] Decree Law 530/1 of May 26, 1961.

[149] In 1927, the Belgians introduced provisions of property law based on those of the Belgian Congo in Book II of the Civil Code. Schabas and Imbleau, *Introduction to Rwandan Law*, p. 95.

[150] Decree Law 09/76 of March 4, 1976.

[151] The National Habitat Policy, adopted December 13, 1996, specifies in Section III, p. 6, that there are two kinds of expropriation, that for the public interest and that "for the benefit of individuals," *pour utilité des particuliers*. In fact, Rwandan law does not recognize this second kind of expropriation for private benefit.

held under customary law, compensation must be paid to the occupant for crops, structures, or other improvements to the land before taking possession of it.[152]

The text of the National Habitat Policy in 1996, as described below, also recognized that occupants must be compensated for land taken by the state.

When establishing imidugudu, authorities confiscated land on which to build the settlements. In addition, they required landholders to "share" land with returnees and, in some cases, to hand over all their land to returnees who claimed to have owned it some decades before. Authorities also took land from cultivators and redistributed it as large-scale holdings to others. In many cases authorities have confiscated land without following the appropriate legal procedures for expropriation and they have not delivered compensation or other plots of land in exchange for the property taken.

Taking the Land

Government officials said repeatedly that grouping dwellings together would make available more land for cultivation. But according to one study, 66 percent of residents in imidugudu say they now have no land while only 47 percent of them were landless before moving to imidugudu. In addition, some 21 percent of the others now have smaller land holdings than they had when living in their old homes.[153] In results only somewhat less negative, a study by government and U.N. agencies reported that only 53 percent of imidugudu residents said they farmed their own land.[154] A study by an independent organization specializing in problems of development looked at the availability of land for residents of imidugudu and concluded: "Very many people do not have any land to grow food or graze animals and those who have it have to walk long distances to work on their land. . . .This situation. . . has exacerbated the poverty that affected most of the imidugudu settlers already. . . ."[155] Dutch researchers also remarked that residents in the imidugudu they studied in Kibungo lacked land even though the region had more land per person than most parts of Rwanda.[156]

Land for the Imidugudu

A substantial number of the newly landless and those with reduced holdings have been deprived of their fields in order to create imidugudu. The Arusha Accords specified that imidugudu were to be located on lands not occupied by individuals.[157] Following that

---

[152]Decree-law no. 21/79, July 23, 1979, article 19.

[153]ADL, *Etude*, p. 36

[154]United Nations, Economic and Social Council, Commission on Human Rights, "Report . . . by the Special Representative, Mr. Michel Moussalli," p. 32.

[155]RISD, "Land Use," paragraph 3.4.1.

[156]Hilhorst and van Leeuwen, "Villagisation in Rwanda," p. 46.

[157]Protocole d'Accord, article 3.

provision, the Ministry for Rehabilitation and Social Integration ordered in December 1994 that only public or state lands could be used for establishing the new settlements. Most early imidugudu were in fact established on public lands, including in a hunting preserve and a national wildlife park, the Akagera Park.[158]

But once the government decreed in December 1996 that all Rwandans would move into imidugudu, it was clear that there was not enough public land available in the country to accommodate all the settlements. At the direction of national authorities, local officials began installing imidugudu on the lands of citizens.

The December 13 text of the National Habitat Policy recognized that landowners whose property was taken for imidugudu must be compensated. It explained in some detail the procedure for expropriating property under Decree-law no. 21/79 of July 23, 1979, including the necessity for compensation to be paid before rights over the land were transferred. It commented that rural as well as urban housing reforms could be slowed if the state had to provide funds to compensate property owners and recommended finding alternative ways to finance the compensation. In the concluding paragraph, the text recommended using public lands for settlement sites because otherwise "It will be necessary to compensate present owners of lands which will be selected as residential sites," which could slow relocation.[159]

When it came to implementing the policy, the government decided that residents of the imidugudu, not the state, would compensate property owners whose land was taken for building sites. An official of the Ministry of Lands, Human Resettlement and Environmental Protection explained: "The state is not able to compensate everyone who is displaced for the villages. The villagers themselves who come [to live on the land] will give compensation. It is up to the people themselves to decide how to do this."[160]

But rarely did the "villagers" deliver any compensation to the person whose land they occupied.[161] One man described what happened in Umutara this way: "Everyone got a piece of land 15 by 30 meters for each family here [in the umudugudu]. We were supposed to give 15 by 30 meters of land in exchange to the other person, but the one who lost the land got nothing and just dropped the matter."[162]

Another cultivator from the same region recounted that 70 meters of the 300 meters of his field had been taken for the site of an umudugudu. "They promised to give me some

---

[158]République Rwandaise, Ministère de Rehabilitation et de Réinsertion Sociale, Problèmes du Repatriement et de la Réinstallation des Réfugiés Rwandais-Proposition de Solutions, December 1994, quoted in Anonymous, "Imidugudu," working document, pp. 7-8.

[159]République Rwandaise, Ministère des Travaux Publics, Politique Nationale de l'Habitat, December 1996, pp. 6-8, 10-11, 22.

[160]Human Rights Watch interviews, Kigali, March 15 and October 23, 2000.

[161]Human Rights Watch interviews, Rutonde and Muhazi, Kibungo, April 15, 1999.

[162]Human Rights Watch interview, Umutara, March 16, 2000.

compensation," he recalled. "But they have not and now I see that the commune has forgotten. It has been two years."[163] Residents of imidugudu in Rutonde and Muhazi communes in Kibungo and of several communes in Ruhengeri told the same story.[164]

In a sample of some 500 imidugudu residents in late 1999, only 8 percent of those who had ceded land for imidugudu received something in exchange. Those fortunate enough to receive plots from others did not necessarily receive land equivalent in value to that lost. And they almost certainly had to travel further to cultivate their fields. The new holdings were necessarily more distant than the fields which had been converted to housing sites and, if they had been given by several people, they might be in widely scattered locations.

Imidugudu residents who moved onto the land of others often sympathized with their plight but themselves had no land or too little land to be able to give compensation. One cultivator from the northwest said: "We are forced to occupy a 20 x 25 meter plot in the umudugudu on land belonging to someone else. We should give him a piece of land of the same size.... It is a big problem for those who do not have land to give in exchange."[165]

In some cases, residents of an umudugudu had land but they refused to compensate the deprived landowner, perhaps because of some past enmity. In one instance, a Tutsi woman whose husband was killed during the genocide refused to give land to compensate a man who had been accused but never convicted of genocide. He had subsequently been released from prison without trial. Indicating the land where her house was located, she said:

> This land belonged to [a man] who lives nearby. Another neighbor is also on his land. He was in prison when we had to move here and he came back to find our houses [on his land]. He couldn't ask for any compensation because he was imprisoned for genocide. I don't know why he was let out of jail. I am not happy to be living next to someone who committed genocide. After his release, he was nice because he was afraid of us, afraid that we would remember what happened.[166]

In most cases, citizens lost crops or structures on the land as well as the land itself. One man from Cyimbogo commune, Cyangugu, lost all the trees which he had planted for harvest and sale. On August 23, 1999, the burgomaster of Mukingo commune in Ruhengeri reportedly ordered land cleared for building a settlement even though crops were in the fields and could have been gathered. Among the six cultivators who lost crops that day was an eighty-year-old man who needed the food for himself and the two orphaned grandchildren who lived with him.[167]

---

[163]Human Rights Watch interview, Umutara, March 16, 2000.

[164]Human Rights Watch interviews, Rutonde and Muhazi, Kibungo, April 15, 1999.

[165]Human Rights Watch interview, Kigali, December 10, 1999.

[166]Human Rights Watch interview, Muhazi, November 30, 1999.

[167]Human Rights Watch interview, Kigali, May 19, 2000. See also RISD, "Land Use," paragraph 4.

"General Sharing Scheme"

The Arusha Accords bound the government to provide land as well as housing for returnees, most of whom were cultivators and pastoralists. In addition to civilians who lived from their herds of cattle, important military officers and RPF leaders owned herds which could number hundreds of cattle. In this they carried on a pattern established during the centuries of Tutsi rule when cattle formed the most important basis for wealth, political power, and social prestige in Rwanda. Following the 1959 revolution and in the face of land scarcity due to population growth, pasture land was largely transformed to crop land. In 1990 few Rwandans inside the country kept more than a few cows and most had none at all. When refugees returned with more than half a million head of cattle, finding pasturage for them added a new dimension to the already difficult issue of land scarcity.

Officials at first allocated public land to the returnees, some of it located in the communes and much of it taken from the Akagera game park and an adjacent hunting preserve. Beginning in 1997 the prefect of Kibungo required landholders in his prefecture to "share" their lands with returnees. This practice, never publicly debated and never sanctioned by law, was soon after implemented elsewhere, including in Umutara and Kigali-rural. Although there was no proclamation of this policy by national authorities, local officials declared that it was imposed from above and that they had no choice but to implement it. They attempted to persuade local residents to divide their land willingly by arguing that returnees had nowhere else to go and that they too had a right to share in the national patrimony.[168]

In many communes, particularly where cultivators owned parcels of two hectares, they divided the land in half and gave one hectare to returnees.[169] Speaking of the situation in Umutara, one man said:

> Each family had a piece of land 300 by 65 meters to start with, but we had to share it with others who needed it. So we had to divide the fields for two families and we were left with 150 by 32.5 meters each.... We didn't understand how we could be made to share land.... But because we had no choice, we kept quiet and shared the land, even though we still don't understand.[170]

In some places, returnees who have received land from one person have later asked more fields from others, sometimes on the prextext of providing for relatives yet to come from abroad. They then rent the fields or have them worked by sharecroppers or paid labor. In other cases, Tutsi returnees have obtained houses and land in imidugudu and then rented the property or even sold it to another. Such efforts to multiply holdings are tolerated by

---

[168] Human Rights Watch interview, Kigali, October 27, 2000.

[169] Human Rights Watch interviews, New York, February 4, 2000; Nyarubuye and Rusumo, Kibungo, June 23, 2000; Nkusi, "Problématique du Régime foncier," p. 18.

[170] Human Rights Watch interview, Umutara, March 16, 2000.

some authorities who fear the returnees and are encouraged by others who are their friends or kin.[171]

In areas where returnees with large herds live near cultivators, such as in Kibungo, the pastoralists sometimes permit their cattle to graze on the crops of the cultivators. Armed with spears and often accompanied by their dogs, they are ready to threaten or even harm cultivators who attempt to protect their fields.[172] According to one genocide survivor these practices and official toleration of them account in part for the flight of some Kibungo residents across the border to Tanzania beginning in April 2000:

> Just imagine how the returnees of 1959 [those who fled Rwanda starting in that year] lead their cattle into fields where there are bananas, sweet potatoes, manioc, corn, and so on, in fields that do not belong to them. When you dare to say anything to them, then you can have a problem. What is unfortunate is that the cattleherders are armed with spears and bring along their dogs to intimidate the owners of the fields. The people complain about this, but the authorities do nothing. So when people see that neither the communal council nor the burgomaster react to this, they decide to leave the country. To hide the real cause, the authorities say they are fleeing *gacaca* when it is not just Hutu who flee but even genocide survivors. . . . My mother is completely overwhelmed. They have burned her stand of banana plants, they have brought their cows to eat her sweet potatoes. In fact the people who were in the country before [i.e., before the arrival of the RPF], we have nothing to say. If I were not here, my mother would already have left for Tanzania.[173]

Such practices as demanding multiple holdings, taking a house and plot of land and then not occupying them, and permitting cattle to destroy the food crops upon which others depend for their subsistence all belie the spirit of sharing so often touted by local officials in trying to spur landholders to divide their fields with the returnees.

"Returning" Property

In both the Arusha Accords and a September 1996 ministerial order, the government asserted the inviolability of property but it in effect guaranteed the same land to two different parties, those—mostly Tutsi—who occupied it before leaving in the first wave of refugees in 1959 and after and those—mostly Hutu—who occupied it before fleeing in the second wave of refugees in 1994. Because the Arusha Accords, which guarantee the property of the

---

[171] Human Rights Watch interviews, Kigali, June 9, 2000; Rusumo, Kibungo, October 29, 2000 and Nyarubuye, Kibungo, October 30, 2000; Hilhorst and van Leeuwen, "Villagisation in Rwanda," pp. 32-33.

[172] Human Rights Watch interview, Kigali, November 1, 2000.

[173] Human Rights Watch, Kigali, October 7, 2000. Gacaca, a term formerly applied to the practice of resolving conflicts by the community, now means the system of popular justice being created by the Rwandan government to prosecute cases of genocide.

Tutsi, were accepted as part of the fundamental law of the land, they presumably carry greater weight than a ministerial order.

Parties to the Accords recommended that returnees not reclaim any property left more than ten years before and now occupied by others, but they obviously could not prohibit them from doing so after having guaranteed the inviolability of property. At first, nonetheless, government officials interpreted this provision as if it were a prohibition, leaving most Rwandans—and many foreigners—convinced that repatriates from the first wave of refugees could not reclaim their property.[174] In 1995, a study by the Ministry of Agriculture together with UNDP found that returnees from the first wave of refugees had not moved onto lands they used to own, particularly when the property was already occupied: "The returnees respect the provisions of the Arusha Accord and are aware that they should not [*ne doivent pas*] reclaim their former properties if they are occupied by other people. They are willing therefore to settle on land other than that of their ancestors."[175] Only exceptionally, such as when the more recent owners had fled or were deceased, did returnees from the first wave of refugees reclaim property abandoned more than ten years before.

The September 1996 ministerial order seemed to confirm the hitherto general practice of favoring more recent occupants over earlier holders of the same property. The order stated that "personal or collective private property cannot be violated," for which position it cited the Rwandan Constitution of June 10, 1991, the June 9, 1993 Arusha protocol on resettlement of refugees, and previous Rwandan decrees and laws on land of 1960 and 1976.[176] After specifying how authorities could grant temporary use of property that had been left by those in flight, it set out the procedure by which a "rightful owner" could reclaim property through local officials. The order stated in article 18, "The legitimate owner of the land is reinstated in his property rights upon his return" and directed local authorities to assist him if the property was not given back within fifteen days of his return.[177]

At the time, the Rwandan government was trying to convince Hutu refugees to come home and it recognized that guaranteeing their rights to the land provided an important

---

[174]Recognition of the property rights of returnees in the Arusha Accord contrasted sharply with the position taken by an earlier government, which in presidential decree no. 25/01 of February 26, 1966 prohibited returnees from claiming land which they inhabited or used previously, if occupied by another. As implemented in its first years, however, the position of the current authorities did not differ substantially from that of the government of the 1960s.

[175]Ephrem Gasasira, "Rwanda, La Question Foncière après la Guerre," République Rwandaise, MINAGRI/PNUD [April 1995], p.16. Nkusi argues that the Arusha Accords amount to expropriation for all who follow the "recommendation," "Problématique du Régime foncier," p. 16.

[176]Republic of Rwanda, Ministerial Order No. 01/96 of September 23, 1996 Regarding the Temporary Management of Land Property.

[177]Ibid.

incentive to return. The order was widely publicized in refugee camps and, according to UNHCR officials, convinced at least some refugees to return to Rwanda.[178]

Unlike cases where Tutsi returnees asserted no claim on the land and ordinarily received part of the property of a landholder at government direction, authorities followed no such simple rule in disputes where returnees claimed that the land had previously belonged to them or their families. As one man who lost land to a Tutsi returnee commented, "What is obscure is the policy. They just leave people to settle it themselves. If only the state said, divide the land this way or that way."[179]

A burgomaster from Gitarama declared that in his commune, where there have been few Tutsi returnees, there had been only one serious conflict over land. Otherwise, he said, "most... just decide to divide it between them."[180] One Hutu in Rusumo who had fled in the second wave of refugees returned to find that Tutsi repatriates from 1959 had simply appropriated his property. "We just shared with the family who had moved in," he said. "They built a house next door to ours. No problem."[181]

But others found no such satisfactory solution. People in several communes of Umutara and Kibungo stated that when they came back from exile in 1996 or after, they found their property occupied by repatriated Tutsi of the first wave of refugees and could not recover it.[182]

The residents of one sector in Nyarubuye commune stated that when they returned from Tanzania in 1997, they found that a large hill which they had cultivated had been converted to pasturage for the cattle of returnees who had moved into the area a year or so before. Those who still had fields divided them with those who had been rendered landless by the appropriation of the returnees.[183]

One Kigali resident with family in Umutara described how Tutsi returnees had reclaimed all their land:

> The people from my family have to work their old fields for the new masters just to be able to eat.... To produce enough food, you have to work all day and then ask the landowner to lend you a little plot on which you can grow your own crops. Most of what you cultivate must go to the others, but at least you can keep the crops you

---

[178]Ibid. An addendum, "Reasons for this Order," suggested that the order was to be made known in refugee camps outside the country, p. 5; Anonymous, "Imidugudu," draft working document, p. 11.

[179]Human Rights Watch interview, Kigali, May 27, 2000.

[180]Human Rights Watch interview, Musambira, Gitarama, August 1, 2000.

[181]Human Rights Watch interview, Rusumo, Kibungo, June 23, 2000.

[182]Human Rights Watch interviews, Rutonde and Muhazi, Kibungo, April 15, 1999.

[183]Human Rights Watch interviews, Nyarubuye, Kibungo, October 30, 2000.

harvest from that little plot.[184]

One man who arrived back in that same area from exile in 1997 was recognized by the returnees who had taken over his property. Because they remembered him fondly from decades before, they lent him a house and allowed him to buy back part of the property in an informal and unregistered transaction.[185]

Land conflicts involving Tutsi returnees have been rare in Ruhengeri because relatively few Tutsi returned there. But two women and a man who were grandchildren of a chief in that area under the colonial administration reportedly displaced twenty-five cultivators from their fields in Kidaho commune in early 2000.[186]

In Cyimbogo, Gisuma, and Gafunza communes, Cyangugu, Tutsi returnees from 1959 have taken some or all of the land occupied by others.[187] Some of the returnees had originally settled in imidugudu in southeastern Rwanda but found conditions there unsatisfactory and returned to Cyangugu to repossess land held by their families decades before.

Tutsi returnees have called on local authorities to back their claims. One local official in Cyangugu explained that people moved to imidugudu in early 2000 after giving over their fields to returnees from 1959. When asked why people had given up their land, he replied, "Because I told them to."[188] An elderly widow who cares for six children and who was one of those coerced into giving up her fields said, "I saw others moving to the umudugudu and, after they took my field away, I thought I had to come here at least to have a plot of land to live on."[189] Others in Cyangugu who felt obliged to turn over all their land to an official whose grandfather had once owned the land also moved to an umudugudu.[190] Another elderly man in Cyimbogo commune decided to hand over virtually all his property to returnees because he feared that otherwise authorities would take reprisals on his son, who had publicly opposed ceding land to repatriates.[191]

---

[184] Human Rights Watch interview, Kigali, May 27, 2000.

[185] Ibid.

[186] Human Rights Watch, "Rwanda: The Search for Security and Human Rights Abuses," A Human Rights Watch Short Report, April 2000, vol. 12, no. 1 (A), p. 22.

[187] Human Rights Watch interviews, Cyimbogo, Cyangugu, May 16 and Cyangugu, May 17, 2000.

[188] Human Rights Watch interview, Cyangugu, May 16, 2000.

[189] Human Rights Watch interview, Cyimbogo, Cyangugu, May 16, 2000.

[190] Human Rights Watch interview, Kigali, November 6, 2000.

[191] Human Rights Watch interview, Kigali, May 19, 2000.

In other cases returnees have called on relatives who are soldiers of the Rwandan Patriotic Army to support their demands for return of their land. One man from Cyangugu said that returnees who were grandchildren of a man who had once owned the land intimidated his brother into ceding all his fields, including some which had been planted with tea, a valuable cash crop: "They came to the house with soldiers who are part of their family. The soldiers have their guns and they say, 'Give us our land back. You know that it is ours.'"[192]

In similar cases in Ruhengeri soldiers of the Rwandan Patriotic Army and government employees have forced cultivators to hand over fields to themselves or members of their families, all of them Tutsi returnees who left the country decades ago.[193]

One man from Cyangugu reported that in his region returnees have aggressively demanded all the holdings they say once belonged to them, a stance that he believed was encouraged by the local political atmosphere. He assessed it this way: "It is the victor and the vanquished. That dominates relations. You spoke yesterday, we speak today. That's how they take the land and say they won't respect Arusha. Habyarimana wrote that and he is now dead. When you dare to challenge this, they consider you a subversive."[194]

Land Taken for Large-Scale Farms

The reorganization of land tenure to favor "modern" farming by "capable professional farmers" has not yet received legislative approval, but such farms have nonetheless been established, depriving hundreds of small-scale cultivators of the land which has been their basis for subsistence. Authorities saw regrouping rural-dwellers in imidugudu as part of the whole process of reorganizing for large-scale farming, although some large holdings have been granted without any direct link to imidugudu.

Holdings of fifty hectares or more in the east and northeast, where the flat, dry grasslands are used to raise cattle, are known as *amarancha* from the English word *ranch*. Other holdings, also primarily for cattle raising, have been carved out of the Gishwati forest in Gisenyi (see below) while farms have been set up in river valleys and marsh lands across the country and are being used for the cultivation of cash crops as well as for stockraising. One expert on land tenure remarked that in some regions the confiscation of land had begun to resemble the enclosure movement in seventeenth and eighteenth century Great Britain.[195]

According to officials of the Ministry of Land, Human Settlement and Environmental Protection, there are established criteria and a procedure for granting these holdings. They say that grantees may receive land only from public or reserve holdings, not from lands held

---

[192]Human Rights Watch interview, Kigali, November 6, 2000

[193]Human Rights Watch, "Rwanda: The Search for Security and Human Rights Abuses," p. 21.

[194]Human Rights Watch, Kigali, May 19, 2000. Habyarimana refers to then President Juvenal Habyarimana, who signed the accords for the Rwandan government.

[195]Nkusi, "Problématique du Régime foncier," p. 26.

by individuals, and that they must pay rent to the state for them. One official at the ministry admitted, however, that powerful persons have dealt directly with local officials and have intimidated them into making grants from the lands of individuals, thus forcibly displacing cultivators.[196] Another highly placed official at the ministry commented in response to an inquiry about land grabbing by military officers, "Individuals do these things. You cannot prevent them from being human beings. But this is not the policy of the government."[197]

One case from Kibungo showed a clear link between the creation of imidugudu and the granting of large holdings of land. One hundred and sixty-six families from the commune of Nyarubuye were forced to leave their homes and fields and move to an umudugudu in an adjacent commune. Their land was then granted to a military officer who used it to pasture his cattle.[198]

In another case in southeastern Kibungo, local residents were forced to leave their homes in a fertile flood plain which was declared a military zone at a time when there were incursions across the border. Military officers later took over the land to grow cash crops and employed the former landholders as wage laborers on the land which used to be theirs. In some cases the military officers, who were absentee landlords, leased the land back to its original occupants. Although there is no longer any immediate threat to security in the region, the original occupants have not been permitted to return to their lands.[199]

In Rusumo commune, local residents report that several extensive grants of land, about twenty hectares each, have been given either to military officers or to wealthy traders or businessmen.[200]

Many extensive amarancha were established in the prefecture of Umutara in the first years after the new government was formed. A cultivator from Umutara related:

> There is a big ranch for cattle near here. The owner is a major in the army. He has been there since sometime after the war of 1994. The fields belonged to the people here before the war but when we came back in 1996, we found the ranch there. We haven't received anything in exchange for our land.[201]

---

[196] Human Rights Watch interviews, Kigali, March 15, 2000.

[197] Human Rights Watch interview, Kigali, October 23, 2000.

[198] Laurent and Bugnion, "External Evaluation of the UNHCR Shelter Program," pp. 44, 96.

[199] Hilhorst and van Leeuwen, "Villagisation in Rwanda," pp. 40-41.

[200] Human Rights Watch interviews, Rusumo, Kibungo, October 30, 2000.

[201] Human Rights Watch interview, Umutara, March 16, 2000.

In one commune in Byumba prefecture, a large farm was established reportedly for the benefit of then President Pasteur Bizimungu and a local official. One man who had previously raised cattle on part of the land said he had received no official notification that the land had been re-assigned by communal authorities. He had heard the news first from other residents of the commune and then had seen it confirmed by the installation of a barbed wire fence around the fields. A woman who had grown crops on a field now enclosed in this farm was no longer allowed to cultivate there and had to borrow a small plot elsewhere to try to grow enough food to feed herself and her family. In March 2000 another powerful person began setting up a farm in the same area, this time on land occupied by homesteads and adjacent fields. The owners of the homes lost all but a minimal plot of land.[202]

In early 2000, a military officer took over a large stretch of land in the Nyabugogo valley, in Butamwa, Kigali-rural, one of the poorest communes in Rwanda. He displaced a number of cultivators who relied on produce from fields in that area for their livelihood. Because of its moisture, the valley was especially valued for cultivating crops in the dry season. The military officer reportedly brought prisoners from Kigali central prison to plant grass on the land and soon after installed his cattle there. Some local officials tried to protect the interests of the cultivators, but the burgomaster supposedly acceded to the demands of the military officer. Most of the people displaced were afraid to protest. But when one threatened to take the matter to the press, the cultivators were given a token payment.[203]

The press reported a case where a group of military officers and businessmen were granted 152 hectares of land being cultivated by some 2,000 people in two communes of Byumba. In a similar case, a sugar-raising enterprise was permitted to displace farmers growing food on 163 hectares in Runda and Shyrongi communes in Gitarama and Kigali-rural prefectures. When the cultivators protested, the government replied that the land belonged to it, not to them and that they should either farm other land or go to work for the company.[204]

In a study of imidugudu done by UNDP and the Rwandan government, respondents from Umutara cited the need for land, "especially the freeing up of marshes monopolized by the owners of farms."[205]

Remedies for the Dispossessed

In the past Rwandans settled property disputes by appealing to the local administrative authority, by resorting to a customary way of resolving conflicts known as gacaca or by taking the case to court. When the government imposed rural reorganization, it did not

---

[202] Human Rights Watch interviews, Kigali and Byumba.

[203] Human Rights Watch interviews, Kigali, June 21 and 27, 2000.

[204] Shyaka Kanuma, "Land Wrangle Displaces 2000 in Byumba," *Rwanda Newsline,* February 14-27, 2000; Victor Visathan, "Squatters on Kabuye Sugar Works land told to quit," *The New Times,* June 7-13, 1999; Radio Rwanda Newsreel, December 12, 2000.

[205] PNUD, *Rapport,* p. 24.

specify any form of recourse for those dissatisfied with the loss of property and relatively few landholders have sought or obtained assistance from the existing mechanisms.

Given that administrative authorities ordinarily were the very persons to impose or support taking the land for imidugudu sites or for redistribution to Tutsi returnees, most of those deprived made no effort to obtain redress from them. A cultivator in Ruhengeri was one of several in his area who had to give up land for an umudugudu and who had received no compensation six months later. He said: "Of course I know the two families who are living on my land. I haven't asked them outright to give me anything. I am waiting for the state to do that. They know about my problem and they haven't offered me anything."[206] When several dissatisfied persons were asked if they had sought a remedy to their complaints from local authorities, they just laughed at the idea. One elderly woman who believed she was unjustly disposessed of her fields commented, "We know this is not the law, but we have nothing to say. We must accept it."[207] One person who worked to defend the interests of cultivators tried unsuccessfully to get authorities to find lands for those whose fields had been taken. "We ask the commune to step in, to give land to the person [deprived]," he said. "But the response is always negative. So the person who lived on the site where the umudugudu has been put is the one who loses."[208]

In a few cases, authorities have created commissions of local residents to try to resolve claims, particularly if they involve a significant number of persons or an important amount of land. This effort to involve the community continues the idea of communal conflict resolution which is the basis of gacaca, but the participation of local authorities in the discussions frequently deprives the group of real autonomy.

Relatively few landholders have tried to reclaim land which they have lost through the courts. The government has dedicated virtually all resources available for the judicial system to prosecuting cases of genocide, more than 100,000 of which await trial, and they have little left for cases involving property disputes. The inexperience of the judges, many of whom are young and minimally trained, and the corruption or susceptibility to political influence which is sometimes charged against them discourages the dissatisfied from filing complaints. In addition, many judges are Tutsi and Hutu often suppose that they would not receive a fair hearing before them.

In some cases those who have sought redress through administrative or judicial channels have obtained relief, but they have been too few and the grounds on which they won too unclear to encourage others to follow suit.[209]

In mid-2000, Rwandan government authorities stepped up efforts to have Tutsi returnees vacate property that belonged to Hutu before 1994, but these efforts mostly

---

[206]Human Rights Watch interview, Ruhengeri, November 18, 1999.

[207]Human Rights Watch interview, Cyimbogo, Cyangugu, May 16, 2000.

[208]Human Rights Watch interview, Kigali, December 10, 1999.

[209]Human Rights Watch interview, Gisuma, Cyangugu, May 16, 2000; cases documented in correspondence from the prefect of Kigali-rural to several burgomasters, 1997-2000; Human Rights Watch interview, Kigali, October 23, 2000.

addressed the illegal occupation of houses and land by those who had no claim on them prior to 1994. In cases where Tutsi returnees claimed land which they said had belonged to them or their families before they fled Rwanda decades ago, the government has not adopted a consistent public position. In a public statement in May 2000, the government stressed that Tutsi returnees had the right to make claims on property they once owned and that the government must enforce such claims if asked to do so.[210] At about the same time, a magistrate said that he and his colleagues had received instructions to begin enforcing such property claims.[211] Yet a document issued in July 2000 by the Ministry of Lands, Human Resettlement and Environmental Protection still took the opposite position, stating that "persons who have been out of the country for ten years or more may not reclaim any previously possessed property."[212]

In the absence of legislative guidance on these complex issues, decisions by officials or the courts are often seen as arbitrary and leave the losing party feeling wronged by authorities as well as by his adversary.[213] A draft document on land policy circulated by officials in November 2000 called on the "government and National Assembly to settle and arrive at an unambiguous interpretation" of the Arusha Accord article 4 concerning the return of property to repatriates who had left the country more than ten years before.[214]

Effect of Land Loss on Cultivators

Those with no land or with insufficient land to sustain themselves and their families survive by cultivating small plots that are borrowed or rented or by working on the land of others, either for pay or in exchange for the right to cultivate a small piece of land for themselves.

A recent mission by the U.N. Office for the Coordination of Humanitarian Affairs, found that imidugudu residents in the region of Bugesera suffered more from food scarcity than others, largely because they had less easy access to land. They found that imidugudu residents, living in conditions like those of a refugee camp, depended on food aid to survive and foresaw that they might remain in such a situation for ten years or more to come.[215] An agricultural expert concluded in a similar though somewhat less drastic vein that food

---

[210]Government of Rwanda, Reply to Human Rights Watch Report, "Rwanda: The Search for Security and Human Rights Abuses," May 2000, posted on the Rwandan government website.

[211]Human Rights Watch interview, Kigali, May 19, 2000.

[212]Government of Rwanda, "Thematic Consultation," p. 12.

[213]Hilhorst and van Leeuwen, "Villagisation in Rwanda," p. 44.

[214]Government of Rwanda, Draft document on land policy, p. 17.

[215]Human Rights Watch interview, Kigali, August 9, 2000; CCA Working Paper, p. 13.

production had declined "because the peasants are not accustomed to this way of organizing the land."[216]

In mid-September 2000, the Food and Agriculture Organisation appealed for increased international food assistance to Rwanda. Remarking that food shortages were in part caused by drought, the announcement stated also that residents of the imidugudu are "especially vulnerable to food shortages."[217]

Some of the cultivators whose land was taken by authorities or with the permission of authorities say that their fields are not now being cultivated. Rather the land is being used for pasturage or is being held for investment purposes. Such a reduction in the amount of land being cultivated would help explain the diminished production noted above.

Opposition to Loss of Land

Those who lost land in the process of creating the imidugudu, in "sharing" with returnees, or in the establishment of large farms suffered enormous hardship but rarely protested openly. One observer remarked, "People are keeping quiet, but they are burning up inside." One cultivator in Ruhengeri said, "Losing my land is really serious but I had no choice but to accept it."[218]

In a small number of reported cases, landholders resisted giving up their fields. In several cases, local officials called in support from the burgomaster or prefect who ordered the resister to comply. In other cases, the recalcitrant were punished, such as in Gisenyi prefecture where two men were jailed in early 2000.[219] In Kibungo prefecture, one woman spent at least a month in jail for refusing to accept the division of her land and a man spent more than fourteen months in jail for having cut down banana trees on a piece of land that he was obliged to give to another.[220] An elderly woman in Kigali-rural was also jailed for three days because she protested having the best part of her land taken by returnees, and others from the same prefecture were reportedly imprisoned for having cultivated on land that was supposedly no longer theirs.[221]

Following the flight of thousands of refugees from Kibungo to Tanzania from April through August 2000, President Kagame went to the region to hear the complaints of local people. Encouraged to speak frankly, they complained of loss of land and encroachment on their fields by pastoralists whose cattle ate their crops. Kagame promptly reproached local officials for permitting such abuses, and in the weeks after, a number of burgomasters and

---

[216]Nkusi, "Problématique du Régime foncier,"p. 32.

[217]United Nations Integrated Regional Information Network, IRIN-CEA Update 1,1018, September 25, 2000.

[218]Human Rights Watch interview, Ruhengeri, November 18, 1999.

[219]Human Rights Watch interview, Gisenyi, March 4, 2000.

[220]Human Rights Watch interviews, November 2 and November 6, 2000.

[221]Human Rights Watch interviews, Kigali, October 27 and November 2, 2000.

the prefect were replaced. It is not yet clear if the changes in personnel will result in any reduction of abuses, but Kagame's visit and the subsequent changes appear to have at least spurred more discussion of land and housing issues and a greater readiness to seek redress for measures which are seen as unfair.[222]

---

[222] Human Rights Watch interview, Kigali, October 26, 2000.

XI. WOMEN, CHILDREN, AND THE ELDERLY

A substantial number of heads of household in imidugudu are drawn from the most vulnerable sectors of society. According to one survey, 59 percent were women, 5 percent were under the age of twenty, and 7 percent were over the age of 60.[223] Given their relative weakness, many had in fact been homeless and unable to obtain property as more powerful people had done. They moved willingly to the new settlements in hopes of having a home. Among them were widows who feared for their security and welcomed the chance to live in a group.[224]

Other women, children, and elderly did have homes and would have preferred to stay in them, but many of them lacked the political or economic power to withstand pressure from authorities and so they too moved quickly to imidugudu.

The order to move has caused many problems for the vulnerable who lack the strength or resources to build new houses. In many imidugudu families headed by women or children occupy the worst structures. One family of five, headed by a woman, live crammed together in a blindé that is some twelve feet long and four feet wide. The oldest daughter in the family is pregnant and expects to raise her child in the same living space. The hangar-like structure is loosely covered with banana leaves that are lifted by passing gusts of wind and that let in the rain in heavy storms. The head of the family explained that when she and others moved to the site, residents able to raise the walls of their houses were given roofing materials to finish the job. But those like herself who lacked the means to build even a simple wood and mud daub house have stayed in blindés.[225]

One widow with three young children from Kinigi commune destroyed her old house and moved to the umudugudu. She had dismantled the roof and brought it along, but it was too old and damaged to keep the rain out, so she used it for makeshift walls and put a piece of plastic sheeting up for a roof. She must travel nearly two miles to fetch water for her family. She would have preferred to stay at home near her field, she said, but she had no choice because the government told her to move to the new settlement. She says she will simply continue surviving this way because she has no power to change the situation. She does not expect to ever have the means to build a solid house again and has, she says, accepted the fact that she will live the rest of her life under plastic sheeting.[226]

In Rutonde commune, Kibungo, a single woman head of household organized other family members to pool their meager resources to build a house for their widowed mother, an elderly genocide survivor. Shortly after they finished the work, the widow was ordered to move to an umudugudu. The daughter said:

This imidugudu policy has caused so many problems for my family—it makes me

---

[223] ADL, *Etude*, p.28.

[224] Human Rights Watch interview, Gisumu, Cyangugu, May 16, 2000.

[225] Human Rights Watch interview, Nyarubuye, Kibungo, October 30, 2000.

[226] Human Rights Watch interview, Kinigi, Ruhengeri, November 19, 1999.

so angry.... Our house was completely destroyed during the genocide. After that, we worked so hard to rebuild it. We really tightened our belts.... And then we had to destroy it. I don't even have a house for myself and my child. And I will have to use all my resources to build another house for my elderly mother in the umudugudu.[227]

In Ruhengeri a local organization had just finished building houses for widows in the commune of Cyeru when the women were ordered to destroy them and move to imidugudu, where they live in blindés covered with banana leaves.[228]

Women heads of household make easy targets for local officials seeking to appropriate land for others. One elderly widow, who cares for six children, was ordered to give all her land to returnees who claimed to be the previous owners. Describing her present situation, she said:

I work for others to get something to eat. Anyone who has work, I do it. Imagine a woman with six children to feed who has no field and needs to beg for work—even though she once had a field.... I get no assistance. We didn't get any material for a roof. The house is not well built and the rain falls on us.

She continued, "A woman cannot get justice in conflicts with a man. We had to accept.... Most of us who had to give fields back [to the returnees] are widows. I know my four neighbors [who gave up land] are widows."[229]

When authorities in Muhazi commune, Kibungo, were appropriating land to give to the landless, they took away virtually all the land of one widow who had complained often and to no avail about being sexually harassed by a brother of a local official. When she saw that the local authorities had put stakes all around her house, leaving her nothing to farm, she again complained but they refused to listen. "Unless you have money for bribes," she said, "you will get nothing."[230]

In Musasa commune, authorities took most of the land of one elderly woman and divided it up for plots for an umudugudu. Plans for construction were then suspended and she was allowed to resume cultivating some of the land. A local official took the rest for his own use and she has not been able to get any help from communal officials in getting it back.[231]

A woman setting up a new household often needed help, a need that left her open to exploitation by local men. "For example," said one women's rights activist, "she needs help

---

[227]Human Rights Watch interview, Rutonde, Kibungo, March 14, 2000.

[228]Human Rights Watch interview, Ruhengeri, December 7, 1999.

[229]Human Rights Watch interview, Cyimbogo, Cyangugu, May 16, 1999.

[230]Human Rights Watch interview, Muhazi, Kibungo, November 30, 1999.

[231]Human Rights Watch interview, Musasa, Kigali-rural, November 7, 2000.

transporting wood for construction. He does it, then comes back at night asking for 'compensation.'"[232]

Local authorities, who ordinarily controlled the distribution of aid, sometimes insisted that women give favors in return for supplies that had been designated for them.[233] One widow in Rutonde commune whose husband was killed during the genocide rebuffed the sexual advances of a local official who then refused to give her the roofing material that was meant for widows like her. She recounted:

> My house was destroyed during the war, but I came back and tried to repair it. A while later they said I had to move to the umudugudu and I did. They were supposed to give me a piece of tin roofing, but I never got any. . . . When you have one problem, other problems follow. You see how sick my children are. They have sores on their heads. I don't know if it's from malnutrition. I don't even have money for soap. . . We have a proverb in Kinyarwanda which says, "Rain falls on everyone, but one person gets more wet." They helped everyone and I am part of the community, but they left me out.[234]

One women's rights activist was outraged when she found local authorities demanding sexual services from women in exchange for roofing materials that had been donated for widows in the Kibungo commune where her family lived. She said: "When they distributed roofing, the authorities gave it to their friends and not to the vulnerable people. If a widow wanted some, the councilor came at night to "photograph" her—that's what they call it, "photograph"—you know, take her *image.*"[235] One genocide survivor, a widow in Kibungo, exclaimed on the vulnerability of women: "We are widows, everywhere! The authorities are men."[236]

Once installed in the settlement, single women caring for young children find the need to travel added distances to get to their fields or to get water or wood especially burdensome. They struggle every day with the problems of taking the children with them to work the fields or of finding some way to leave them safely at home.[237]

Children who head households also suffer hardship because authorities find it easy to take property away from them. One slight thirteen-year-old in Rusumo commune, Kibungo, struggles to feed his siblings, aged twelve and eight, and his elderly grandmother. There is

---

[232]Human Rights Watch interview, Rwamagana, Kibungo, November 24, 1999.

[233]"Nothing will be white as snow," *Imvaho Nshya*, no. 129, July 26-August 1, 1999.

[234]Human Rights Watch interview, Rutonde, Kibungo, March 14, 2000.

[235]Human Rights Watch interview, Rwamagana, Kibungo, March 14, 1999.

[236]Human Rights Watch interview, Muhazi, Kibungo, November 25, 1999.

[237]Human Rights Watch interviews and observations, Cyimbogo, Cyamgugu, May 16, 2000.

no money to pay school fees, so none of the children attends school. Their parents were killed in the war and their land was later taken to serve as the site for the umudugudu. In exchange, they were allocated a field that is some seven miles distant. Each day in the growing season, the thirteen-year-old makes the fourteen mile round trip on foot, using what is left of his time and energy to cultivate the field. Inside the small blindé that serves as their home, there is no furniture and only a few grass mats to serve as bed and covers.[238]

The elderly also often suffer greatly from having to move to imidugudu. Seven of twelve persons who had to destroy their homes in one cell of a Ruhengeri commune were over the age of sixty and one was an eighty-year-old woman. Half of the cultivators who had their crops destroyed when land was cleared for a building site in another cell of the same commune were over the age of sixty.[239]

In some cases local officials organized other residents to help the weak and elderly. In others religious or humanitarian organizations mustered workers to help build houses. But given the scarcity of resources for most in the imidugudu, the neediest could not rely on help being either abundant or long-term.[240]

---

[238]Human Rights Watch interview, Rusumo, Kibungo, October 29, 2000.

[239]Human Rights Watch interview, Kigali, May, 2000.

[240]Human Rights Watch interviews, Rutonde and Muhazi, Kibungo, April 15, 1999; Cyimbogo, Cyangugu, May 16, 2000.

XII. RECONCILIATION

Once Rwandan authorities grafted the imidugudu policy onto internationally-funded housing programs, they began frequently citing reconciliation as one of the objectives of the policy. They asserted that relocating all rural-dwellers and obliging landholders to divide their land with returnees was essential to avoiding conflict between groups. These measures may have avoided some disputes in the short-term but have laid the grounds for longer-term conflict now taking shape among citizens and between citizens and the authorities.[241]

Officials early on acknowledged the risks of having Tutsi returnees and survivors of genocide living in imidugudu apart from the surrounding Hutu population. They have cited these risks in explaining the importance of moving all the rest of rural-dwellers into settlements as well. But relatively few of the imidugudu created so far are ethnically mixed. A report published in September 1999 concluded that "in most cases" the imidugudu comprised people of a single ethnic group, an assertion confirmed by observations of Human Rights Watch researchers.[242] A UNHCR evaluation team reported that twenty of twenty-nine imidugudu which they visited in late 1999 were inhabited by people of one ethnic group.[243] The move to imidugudu may even have promoted ethnic segregation by disturbing previously existing housing patterns, which were often ethnically diverse.

In those imidugudu which were ethnically mixed, the resources available to Hutu were often much less than those available to Tutsi, a difference which exacerbated tensions in some cases. In Bicumbi commune, near Kigali, Tutsi returnees live on one side of the road in solid adobe brick houses, coated with cement and with strong roofs, built with UNHCR funds. Hutu from the surrounding area, who moved to the settlement later, are clustered on the other side of the road in shelters of wood, mud, and plastic sheeting. One resident said she thought that the houses were different "because they are Tutsi and we are not."[244] The same situation, complete with ill-feeling between those who had received different levels of assistance, was reported by UNHCR evaluators for imidugudu in Kagabiro, Kibuye prefecture.[245]

An elderly woman in Ruhengeri explained that when she moved, as she was told she would have to do shortly, she did not expect any help from the authorities. She laughed and said:

Only "those who own the country" (*bene 'gihugu*) get assistance. . . You know, those who left in 1959, like those who live in Kimonyi umudugudu in Mukingo

---

[241]RISD, "Land Use," paragraph 3.4.2; Hilhorst and van Leeuwen, "Villagisation in Rwanda," p. 46.

[242]RISD, "Land Use," paragraph 3.4.2.

[243]Laurent and Bugnion, "External Evaluation of the UNHCR Shelter Program," p. xi.

[244]Human Rights Watch interview, Bicumbi, Kigali-rural, October 26, 2000.

[245]Laurent and Bugnion, "External Evaluation of the UNHCR Shelter Program," p. xi.

commune.... If you want [to see the difference], go to Kinigi near the forest. There are people in sheeting and grass there. When the rain falls, it falls on them, even though they had solid houses before! We are waiting to be like those in Kinigi. If they didn't give assistance to Kinigi, our case will doubtless be like theirs.[246]

One woman in the northwest still living in the solid home in which she invested all her savings, spoke bitterly of the order to destroy the only property she has left after years of war: "People are very sad. This is an act of revenge. It is a vengeance. There is a local official who supposedly said '[Tutsi] left in 1959 and their homes were destroyed then. Why don't you want to destroy yours?' People see this as a subtle form of vengeance."[247]

According to foreign experts who keep track of assistance provided to residents of imidugudu, settlements inhabited by Tutsi returnees and survivors of the genocide ordinarily received more services, such as health care, as well as better housing.[248]

In July 2000 members of the Twa ethnic group, a minority which now amounts to less than one percent of the population, complained that they received even fewer benefits than other Rwandans under the imidugudu policy. Historically scorned by both Hutu and Tutsi, they rarely received land or houses in the new settlements.[249]

In some cases, Tutsi received more or better resources than Hutu because donors had designated returnees or survivors of genocide as recipients of their aid. In other cases donors specified that aid was to go to all needy persons, but local residents—mainly Hutu—moved to imidugudu after the resources were largely exhausted. While some obtained at least roofing materials, the most expensive item for building a house, others came when there was nothing left and had to make do with a piece of plastic sheeting. Officials occasionally tried to remedy the situation by pressing higher authorities for aid or by trying to create local mechanisms for assistance. In early 2000 the then prefect of Gisenyi, for example, told a Human Rights Watch researcher that he tried to establish a small operation to produce cheap roofing materials for those now living under plastic sheeting.[250]

Many Hutu believe that they have lost more from the imidugudu policy than have Tutsi, but there are cases where Tutsi too have suffered extreme hardship. In addition to those mentioned above, two groups of returnees attracted considerable attention for the hardship they endured in 2000.

---

[246]Human Rights Watch interview, Ruhengeri, May 26, 2000.

[247]Human Rights Watch interview, Kigali, November 27, 1999.

[248]Human Rights Watch interview, Kigali, May 25, 2000.

[249]Human Rights Watch interviews, Kigali, July 11, 2000; United Nations Integrated Regional Information Network, Great Lakes, Focus on the Twa People, July 5, 2000.

[250]Human Rights Watch interview, Gisenyi, January 14, 2000.

Reconciliation

More than 12,000 Tutsi returnees from the Congo were settled in the Gishwati forest beginning in 1995 "to help the army protect security."[251] They were expected to occupy the uninhabited regions and make it less likely that insurgents could establish bases there. Subsequently cattleowners from elsewhere in the country sent their herds to the well-watered and productive forest area, reputed to be excellent for cattle-raising. A parliamentary commission investigated the increasing cattle population and the damage to the forest, one of the rare stands left in Rwanda. Officials decided to move the people. In late 1999, the minister of local government ordered the families to leave the land they had cleared and cultivated. For months, authorities offered virtually no assistance and the displaced people huddled in plastic tents in several camps. In August 2000 the government offered them new places to settle in several northwestern communes. The officials said they decided to remove the families because they became aware of the damage being done to the natural environment. Some of the displaced, echoed by the press, questioned if this were the reason—or, in any case, the only reason—for the decision. They said that the large herds of cattle belonging to important people in the prefectural and national capital remained in the forest and grew fat, in part from eating the crops they were forced to leave behind.[252]

In a second case, some Tutsi returnees who settled originally in the southeast later moved to Cyangugu where they arrived too late to benefit from the original generous support to repatriates. Most obtained no fields and received food assistance only occasionally. One elderly man who headed a household that included his wife and eight others, including three widowed daughters and their children, recounted what happened when the commune announced that it was preparing a list of the needy. Seventy-four families asked to be listed, but officials insisted that only twenty names could be taken. He continued,

> We live like that. It is God who keeps us alive. Like birds that fly in the air.
> And help we get from others, those who come with a little food for us.
> I don't know how we happened to get aid this month. Since we are not
> strong enough to struggle with the crowd to get beans, we yelled at them
> to help and they helped us. . . . They decided to give us two kilo of beans.
> Imagine two kilo of beans for a family of ten! It is not enough for even
> two people.[253]

---

[251] Jean Baptiste Mugunga, "Cry of Alarm at Gishwati," *Journal Rushyashya*, no. 15, December 1999.

[252] Ibid.; Human Rights Watch interviews, Gisenyi, March 4, 2000; Badege Aloys Habimana, "Wisdom Needed for the Gishwati Case" and "8500 Hectares in Gishwati Can Be Inhabited," *Imvaho Nshya*, no. 1319, January 17-23, 2000, pp. 6-8.

[253] Human Rights Watch interview, Kamembe commune, Cyangugu, May 17, 2000.

In early 2000 the severely malnourished received some food from churches and religious congregations, but not nearly enough.[254] According to news reports on Radio Rwanda, ten people died of hunger in this area in late January and another 4,400 were at risk because of severe malnutrition in September.[255]

In interviews with Human Rights Watch researchers, residents of imidugudu expressed anger at government authorities, both for imposing the rural reorganization and for instances of corruption related to it. They complained about the as yet unresolved accusations of corruption at the national level which may have deprived them of needed assistance.[256] Others recounted with disgust the corruption that they have seen at local level. In an umudugudu near the offices of Muhazi commune, for example, soldiers, communal policemen, and administrative officials used local detainees to make adobe bricks for new houses which they apparently intended to occupy or rent to others. They roofed the houses with materials provided by international assistance. Tutsi and Hutu residents of the umudugudu, whether returnees, genocide survivors, or others, did not dispose of such free abundant labor and they built their houses more slowly. By the time they were ready to ask for roofing materials, there were none left. As a result, some of the residents have lived more than two years in blindés covered with grass.[257] Elsewhere citizens and the press accused local officials of having taken bribes to allocate lands in or around imidugudu, of having distributed houses or larger plots of lands to favorites, and of having excused others from having to give land to serve as settlement sites.[258]

The loss of resources, conflicts over land, the inhumane conditions of life, and the growing hunger all have exacerbated fear and anger, hardly conditions likely to promote reconciliation.

---

[254]Human Rights Watch interview, Cyangugu, May 16, 2000.

[255]Radio Rwanda, news reports, January 21-23, September 7, 2000.

[256]See *Rwanda Newsline*, March 13-36, 2000 for accounts of accusations against the Ministry of Rehabilitation and Social Reinsertion; Niyonsaba Anselme, "Commune Rutongo: Communal Authorities Work Poorly," *Ukuri*, 97, vol. 2, March 1999.

[257]Human Rights Watch interviews and observations, Muhazi, Kibungo, April 15, 1999.

[258]Human Rights Watch interview, Gisenyi, October 30, 1999. For an example, see Isaie Karangwa, "Serious Problems with Land in Muvumba Commune," *Ukuri*, vol. 2, March 1999; also RISD, "Land Use," paragraph 3.2.3.1 and paragraph 4.

XIII. NUMBERS

Returnees from the First Wave of Refugees, 1959-1973

The Rwandan government has often presented the imidugudu policy as a reaction to a housing crisis of overwhelming proportions. It is certainly true that there were hundreds of thousands of persons needing shelter in late 1996, but Rwandan authorities have sometimes exaggerated the extent of the crisis. In a speech referred to below, for example, President Paul Kagame talked of four million people who needed to be settled. A realistic estimate of the numbers of homeless is relevant to assessing the context in which the government acted and its supposed justification for forcing people into imidugudu.

The government generally asserts that nearly 800,000 refugees of the first wave of departures—that is, those who fled between 1959 and 1973—have returned to Rwanda, virtually all of them by late 1996 or early 1997. This figure rests upon an undocumented government estimate of 600,000 returnees in 1994, to which was added 175,000 counted as returning by UNHCR in 1995 and 1996. Another 21,000 returnees were counted by UNHCR from 1997 to 1999, to bring the total to 796,000 at the end of 1999, a figure usually rounded up to 800,000.[259]

But experts from the U.N. Fund for Population and demographers from the Rwandan government National Population Office who prepared a socio-demographic survey at the end of 1996 commented that their data "would corroborate the view that some over-estimation of 'old returnees' [i.e., those who left between 1959 and 1973] could have occurred."[260] This comment drew little attention, which is remarkable given that these numbers have been used as the basis for allocating millions of dollars in aid. According to the survey, only 5.2 percent of Rwandans present in the country at the end of 1996, or some 321,000 persons, said they had been born abroad. In addition to these persons, the category of "old returnees" includes also those born in Rwanda who later became refugees and then came home. Unfortunately the demographers did not publish any statistics for this group, although they may have had them.[261]

Data on the number of Rwandans living outside the country just before the war, however, corroborates the suggestion that 796,000 is too high a number for the "old returnees." According to information from UNHCR, 379,000 Rwandans were refugees

---

[259] Republic of Rwanda and United Nations Population Fund, *Socio-Democraphic Survey 1996*, p. 31; Government of Rwanda, Ministry of Lands, Human Resettlement and Environmental Protection, "Thematic Consultation," p. 2.

[260] Republic of Rwanda and United Nations Population Fund, *Socio-Democraphic Survey 1996*, p. 31.

[261] The report refers to its data on "previous residence" abroad, but does not publish any such data. Republic of Rwanda and United Nations Population Fund, *Socio-Democraphic Survey 1996*, p. 31. When contacted with a request for further information on these questions, the foreign expert who worked on the report replied only that these were "sensitive" issues.

outside the country in 1990. Other data on the total number of Rwandans living in neighboring countries in 1992, both officially declared refugees (who would be counted by UNHCR) and others, puts that figure at about 600,000.[262] Even if every one of these people had decided to return to Rwanda, the number would be nearly 200,000 short of the usually cited figure of 800,000 "old returnees."

Given these facts, the estimate of 800,000 should be regarded with some skepticism until the government conducts a reliable census and determines how many persons now living in Rwanda were refugees who left between 1959 and 1973.

Imidugudu Residents

It is important to know how many people live in imidugudu in order to assess the impact of this program on the lives of Rwandans, yet it is difficult to obtain reliable data on this subject. In late 1999, a study by UNDP together with the Rwandan government estimated that some 177,000 new houses had been completed in imidugudu since 1994 and that 134,024 of them were occupied.[263]

These figures may have been somewhat inflated. UNHCR, the most important source of aid, built or provided materials to build some 85,000 houses.[264] In addition, UNDP supported the building of about 20 percent of the total, which indicates that the number built was some 108,000.[265] In addition, some construction was financed directly by bilateral donors. Taking into account the fact that some houses were built outside imidugudu, we would conservatively estimate that some 100,000 houses were completed and occupied in imidugudu.

The UNDP-Rwandan government study concluded that about 117,000 households were living in imidugudu in unfinished houses or shelters roofed with plastic sheeting or grass. This figure did not include data from the prefecture of Ruhengeri, where information was not collected due to insecurity at the time of the study and where many were still in inadequate housing. In late 1999, for example, some 14,500 households in the single commune of Kinigi had moved into imidugudu and most of them were still in temporary shelters.[266] Allowing for some exaggeration, a conservative estimate based on this data

---

[262]André Guichaoua, "Vers Deux Générations de Réfugiés Rwandais," pp. 341 and 343, in André Guichaoua, *Les Crises Politiques au Burundi et au Rwanda* (Lille: Université des Sciences et Technologies de Lille, 1995). See also UNHCR, *Refugees and Others of Concern to UNHCR, 1999 Statistical Overview*, Table 11.7.

[263]PNUD, *Rapport,* pp.6-8.

[264] CCA Working Paper no. 3, note p. 3. UNHCR statistics are discussed below.

[265]Human Rights Watch interview, Kigali, August 15, 2000.

[266] PNUD, *Rapport,* p.8; Human Rights Watch interview, Kinigi, Ruhengeri, November 19, 1999; Government of Rwanda, "Thematic Consultation," p. 2.

would be that at least 125,000 households were then living in temporary shelters or unfinished houses in imidugudu.[267]

If 100,000 households were living in completed houses and another 125,000 were in temporary shelters or unfinished houses, this would mean that 225,000 households were in imidugudu at the end of 1999. Using the figure of 4.8 persons per household established by the 1996 socio-demographic survey this equates to 1,080,000 people living in the settlements at that time.[268] In the ensuing year, an undetermined number, but certainly thousands more, have moved to the settlements.

One expert on rural life using other data estimated that just under one million people had moved to imidugudu.[269]

Given the unreliability of date, it is currently impossible to arrive at an exact number of residents in imidugudu and even more impossible to be sure how many of them are living there against their will, but these figures give an idea of the scale of the numbers involved. At the least hundreds of thousands of people have moved to the settlements; at the least tens of thousands of them have been displaced against their will and many of those have been compelled to destroy their own homes.

---

[267]To appreciate how conservative these estimates are, compare Rwandan government estimates. In January 2000, it said 625,000 persons (125,000 households) had been moved from camps to imidugudu in the the two northwestern prefectures and that some 163,000 persons (32,600 households) lived in completed houses, which would leave 462,000 persons (92,400 households) in temporary shelters for Ruhengeri and Gisenyi. According to the November 1999 data, Gisenyi represented only some 3,100 households of this total. CCA Working Paper, no. 3, pp. 8, 10.

[268]Republic of Rwanda and United Nations Population Fund, *Socio-Democraphic Survey 1996*, p. 41. The relative numbers in finished houses, unfinished houses, or shelters will have changed since the data was collected in late 1999, but this will not have affected the total number of residents.

[269]Human Rights Watch interview, Kigali, by telephone, September 11, 2000.

XIV. VIOLATIONS OF HUMAN RIGHTS

The Rwandan National Habitat Policy violates provisions of international human rights law on several counts. The Universal Declaration of Human Rights is directly incorporated into article 17 of protocol VII of the Arusha Accords, now part of the fundamental law of Rwanda. Rwanda has also ratified the International Covenant of Civil and Political Rights (ICCPR), the International Covenant on Economic, Social and Cultural Rights (ICESCR), and the African Charter of Human and Peoples' Rights.[270]

Right to Freedom of Movement and Choice of Residence

The ICCPR at article 12 declares that everyone shall have "the right to liberty of movement and freedom to choose his residence."[271] Commentators widely agree that incorporated in the freedom of residence is the right not to be moved.[272] As noted at article 12 (3), restrictions on the freedoms of movement and residence are permitted only when provided by law and for reasons of "national security, public order (*ordre public*), public health or morals, or the rights and freedoms of others." Such restrictions must also be consistent with other rights recognized by the ICCPR. Article 12(4) specifies that movement and residence may also be restricted during an officially proclaimed public emergency.

Various U.N. bodies have further defined this right. In a 1997 resolution, the Sub-Commission on Prevention of Discrimination and Protection of Minorities of the U.N. Commission on Human Rights affirmed "the right of persons to remain in their own homes, on their own lands, and in their own countries. . . ." It also urged governments and other actors to do everything possible "to cease at once all practices of forced displacement [and] population transfer. . . in violation of international legal standards."[273]

In another resolution in 1997, the Sub-Commission reaffirmed the right "not to be evicted arbitrarily. . . from one's home, land or community." It noted that "coerced and involuntary removal" of persons from their homes and lands could result in "greater

---

[270]Schabas and Imbleau, *Introduction to Rwandan Law*, pp. 161-70.

[271]The African Charter at article 12(1) also recognizes this right.

[272]See Patrick McFadden, "The Right to Stay," *Vanderbilt Journal of Transnational Law,* vol. 29, p. 36 (1966).

[273]United Nations, Economic and Social Council, Commission on Human Rights, Sub-Commission on Prevention of Discrimination and Protection of Minorities, "Freedom of Movement and Population Transfer," E/CN.4/SUB.2/RES/1997/29. See also United Nations, Economic and Social Council, Commission on Human Rights, "Further Promotion and Encouragement of Human Rights and Fundamental Freedoms Including the Question of the Programme and Methods of Work of the Commission, Questions of Human Rights, Mass Exoduses and Displaced Persons, Report of the Representative of the Secretary-General, Mr. Francis Deng, Addendum, Compilation and Analysis of Legal Norms, Part II: Legal Aspects Relating to the Protection Against Arbitrary Displacement, E/CN.4/1998/53/Add.1, Section II, A, paragraph 4. Hereafter cited as "Report of Mr. Francis Deng. . .Part II."

homelessness and inadequate housing and living conditions. . . .," an observation that fits the Rwandan case well. It also noted that for an eviction to be considered justifiable would require that it not be carried out arbitrarily but through legal procedures that ensure appropriate due process protections. Arbitrariness may be presumed from widespread displacement where cases have not been examined on an individual basis.

The Sub-Commission stated that to be permissible, an eviction "must not result in individuals being rendered homeless or vulnerable to other human rights violations." It recommended that governments provide "immediate restitution, compensation and/or appropriate and sufficient alternative accomodation or land" to those who had been forcibly evicted from their homes.[274] This was not done for most who lost land in Rwanda.

In some cases, the Rwandan government used force or the threat of force to compel rural-dwellers to move to designated sites. It punished those who refused to comply by fines or imprisonment. In many more cases, it coerced people into relocating, the test of coercion being whether or not those concerned had a "real choice" whether to go or to stay.[275] As is clear from statements of witnesses quoted above, many people believed—and some had been expressly told by authorities—that they had no such choice and were required to move by "law." By forcing Rwandans to leave their homes and by compelling them to live at designated sites rather than on their own lands, or elsewhere that they might choose, the government violated their right to chose their residence.

States may only restrict the right to freedom of movement and of choice of residence under certain circumstances and as provided by law.[276] According to the Rwandan constitution and the Arusha Accords, laws are adopted by the Transitional National Assembly or by the Cabinet and then promulgated by the president within ten days of their approval by the Constitutional Court.[277] The National Habitat Policy which requires the relocation of all rural-dwellers to imidugudu was not established by this procedure but resulted from a simple decision by the Cabinet which was implemented by two ministerial orders, one of them a provisional order.

Rwandan authorities and others have sometimes asserted that the Arusha Accords provide a legal basis for the establishment of imidugudu.[278] At a meeting with international agencies in January 1997, Minister of Rehabilitation and Social Integration Patrick

---

[274]United Nations, Economic and Social Council, Sub-Commission on Prevention of Discrimination and Protection of Minorities, Forced Evictions, E/CN.4/SUB.2/RES/1997/6.

[275]"Report of Mr. Francis Deng. . .Part II," paragraph 3.

[276]ICCPR, Article 12 (3).

[277]Schabas and Imbleau, *Introduction to Rwandan Law*, p. 15.

[278]Republique Rwandaise, Ministère des Terres, de la Réinstallation, et de la Protection de l'Environment, "Habitat en Milieu Rural," article 2, La Politique de l'Habitat en Milieu Rural, June 1999; Anonymous, "Imidugudu, Assessment of Housing and Land Reform Plans in Rwanda," May 1997, draft working document and appended texts, p. 14 ; Nkusi, "Problématique du Régime foncier," p.26.

Mazimhaka reportedly maintained that plans for the imidugudu "are an outcome" of the Arusha Accords.[279] A working paper on resettlement prepared in January 2000 stated that "The current policy on resettlement in rural areas is based on the Arusha agreement."[280]

But the Accords specified only that returnees were to be resettled in "villages" and made no reference to living patterns of other Rwandans.[281]

In addition, the Accords guaranteed refugees who returned to Rwanda the right to settle in a place of their choice, provided they did not violate the rights of others. By compelling them to live in imidugudu, the government violated its own law as provided in protocol V, article 2, of the Accords.

The Rwandan government often sought to justify the necessity to move to imidugudu on the grounds of "national security," particularly in the northwest just after the insurgency. Even at that time, such a justification had little merit; any semblance of need for such measures in the interest of national security has long since ended. The Rwandan government itself has said that it has suppressed the insurgency and driven the insurgents from the country.[282] Any restriction of freedom to choose one's residence because of national security is permissible only for the duration of the crisis and so is necessarily temporary. But the Rwandan government has stated clearly that relocation to imidugudu is meant to be permanent. Nor do any of the other possible justifications for restricting this right apply in this case.

Right to Adequate Housing

The ICESCR provides at article 11 (1) for "the right of everyone to an adequate standard of living for himself and his family, including adequate food, clothing and housing." The problem of forced evictions figures prominently in international debate on adequate housing. In 1991 the U.N. Committee on Economic, Social, and Cultural Rights stated that "forced evictions are prima facie incompatible with the requirements of the

---

[279] Notes of the meeting provided by a diplomat in Kigali.

[280] CCA Working Paper No. 3, p. 3.

[281] Protocole d'Accord, article 28.

[282] See, for example, Government of Rwanda, Reply to Human Rights Watch Report, "Rwanda: The Search for Security and Human Rights Abuses," May 2000, posted on the Rwandan government website.

Covenant."[283] Likewise the U.N. Commission on Human Rights in 1993 concluded that "forced evictions are a gross violation of human rights."[284]

The Committee on Economic, Social, and Cultural Rights has defined forced evictions as "the permanent or temporary removal against their will of individuals, families and/or communities from the homes and/or land which they occupy, without the provision of, and access to, appropriate forms of legal or other protection."[285] Noting that the obligation of states to use "all appropriate means" to enforce economic and social rights, as specified in ICESCR article 2 (1), will rarely be relevant in cases of forced eviction, the Committee concluded that the state itself "must refrain from forced evictions and ensure that the law is enforced against its agents or third parties who carry out forced evictions."[286]

According to the Committee, forced evictions involve a large number of rights recognized by both international human rights covenants in addition to the right to adequate housing.[287] It found, therefore, that appropriate procedural protections and due process were especially necessary. Such procedural protections include genuine consultation with those affected, providing them with timely information about the proposed evictions and the use to which the land or housing is to be put, and providing them with legal remedies, including legal aid to persons who are in need of it to seek redress from the courts.[288]

The Guiding Principles on Internal Displacement, which reflect international human rights and humanitarian law, are also relevant to the rural resettlement program. They state that the arbitrary displacement of persons is prohibited in cases of "large-scale development projects, which are not justified by compelling and overriding public interest."[289] The Guiding Principles add that authorities must explore "all feasible alternatives" to avoid displacement. If there is no possible alternative, then they must take all measures to minimize displacement and its adverse effects, including assuring the procedural protections just mentioned.[290] According to the Guiding Principles, "states are under a particular

---

[283] United Nations, Committee on Economic, Social and Cultural Rights, General Comment No. 4 (1991) of the Committee on Economic, Social and Cultural Rights on the right to adequate housing (art. 11 (1) of the Covenant), December 12, 1991, paragraph 18. See generally U.N. Commission on Human Rights, Fact Sheet no. 25, Forced Evictions and Human Rights, 1996.

[284] U.N. Commission on Human Rights, Resolution 1993/77, paragraph 1.

[285] U.N. Committee on Economic, Social, and Cultural Rights, Right to Adequate Housing (Art. 11.1), forced evictions, General Comment no. 7, 1997, paragraph 3.

[286] Ibid., paragraph 8.

[287] Ibid., paragraph 9.

[288] Ibid., paragraph 15.

[289] The Guiding Principles on Internal Displacement, section 2, principle 6(c).

[290] Ibid., principle 7.

obligation to protect against the displacement of... peasants, pastoralists and other groups with a special dependency on and attachment to their lands."[291]

Right to Secure Enjoyment of One's Home

Article 17 of the ICCPR provides protection against "arbitrary or unlawful interference" with a person's "privacy, family, home or correspondence." In addition to abstaining from interfering with this right, parties to the covenant assume the responsibility to actively protect it.[292] According to international legal commentators, "home" here means not just a dwelling but any residential property, regardless of legal title or nature of use. Any activity that deprives one of his or her home represents interference which must be decided by the authority designated under law and on a case-by-case basis.[293]

Rwandan law further protects the home against intrusion, which to be legitimate must be authorized by law.[294]

In implementing the policy of imidugudu, officials of the state required people to abandon and even to destroy their dwellings, depriving at the very least tens of thousands of people of their homes.

Right to Freedom of Opinion and of Expression

The ICCPR, at article 19, guarantees the right to hold opinions without interference and to express them freely. Although some newspapers published criticism of abuses related to imidugudu without suffering any ill consequence, local people who spoke out against the habitat policy or the appropriation of their lands were in several cases imprisoned, fined, or otherwise punished for holding these views and for expressing them.

Right to Property

The right to property, recognized by article 17 of the Universal Declaration of Human Rights, is also guaranteed by the Rwandan constitution. According to Rwandan law, this right may be limited only in cases of public utility, as provided by law. Any expropriation must be preceded by prior and fair compensation.[295]

Government officials deprived cultivators of their land in order to create imidugudu. Most received no compensation for this land. If they did receive other land, it was often not of equivalent value, because the soil was poorer, because the field was more distant, or because the holdings were dispersed in several locations and so less efficient to farm. In some cases, government officials confiscated or allowed others to confiscate the land of

---

[291] Ibid., principle 9.

[292] "Everyone has the right to the protection of the law against such interference....", ICCPR, article 17 (2).

[293] "Report of Mr. Francis Deng...Part II," Section II, B, paragraphs 1 and 2.

[294] Schabas and Imbleau, pp. 178-9.

[295] Decree law no. 21/79 of July 23, 1979. Schabas and Imbleau, p. 179.

Rwandans without compensation or appropriate procedure in order to create large-scale farms. According to international legal opinion, people who depend on the land for their very survival, as do more than 90 percent of Rwandans, are entitled to special protection of their right to the land.[296]

Right to Remedy

The ICCPR at article 2 (3a) guarantees the right to "an effective remedy" for those whose rights are violated. Rwandans whose rights to choice of residence, to adequate housing, to undisturbed enjoyment of their homes, to freedom of expression, and to security of property have been violated do not ordinarily and regularly have access to an effective remedy. Some have successfully pleaded their cases, often through the use of personal or political ties, but the opportunity of the few to obtain satisfaction through such irregular means does not meet the standard of effective remedy required by this article of the ICCPR.

---

[296]"Report of Mr. Francis Deng. . .Part II," section 3, paragraph 4.

XV. THE ROLE OF THE INTERNATIONAL COMMUNITY

International donors and humanitarian agencies provided generous assistance to build houses for Rwandans who had none—and who were grateful for the help—but some of their aid was used to create imidugudu to which rural-dwellers were forced to move against their will. In an ironic twist, the program which donors supported in hopes of ending homelessness covered another which caused tens of thousands of Rwandans to lose their homes. Praise for the generosity and promptness with which donors responded to the housing program must be tempered by criticism of their readiness to ignore the human rights abuses occasioned by the rural reorganization program that operated under its cover.

In late 1996 international actors had several reasons to feel guilty about their behavior towards Rwandans. Not only had they failed to end the 1994 genocide, they had also refused to halt the rearming and reorganizing of genocidal forces in the refugee camps in Zaire. Once the Rwandan army and their allies in Zaire began attacking the camps, international actors made a feeble, short-lived effort to organize a military force to assist civilians. But they rapidly backed down when the Rwandan troops destroyed the camps and then stood by—largely in silence—while the Rwandan and allied forces chased down and slaughtered refugees who did not return promptly to Rwanda. The U.S., among others, blocked efforts by UNHCR to protect the refugees and contested their reports about the numbers who had fled into the Zairean forests. Other governments less closely identified with the Rwandan government understood that the slaughter of tens of thousands of persons was being covered up, but took no effective action to challenge the pretense that all real refugees—those not associated with genocidal militia or soldiers—had returned to Rwanda.[297]

Donors

With the return of the refugees, the need for housing was clear. Meeting that need allowed international actors to demonstrate their support for the Arusha Accords while also assuaging the guilt they felt—whether towards Tutsi or Hutu, or both. As the UNDP representative wrote in a discussion paper in January 1997:

> The current shelter construction programme is important, not only in itself but also as a tangible symbol of international assistance which is important both for the Government and for donors. The physical construction of housing will become a visible benchmark of the effectiveness of international assistance, and as such will assume an importance over and beyond the meeting of housing needs.[298]

---

[297] See Human Rights Watch, "What Kabila is Hiding: Civilian Killings and Impunity in Congo," October 1997, Vol. 9, No. 5 (A).

[298] Discussion Paper, "Shelter, Settlement and Beyond. . ." enclosed in Omar Bakhet, UNDP Resident Representative and U.N. Resident Coordinator, to Ambassadors and Charge d'Affaires, Heads of U.N. Agencies, January 23, 1997. Emphasis in the original.

When Rwandan officials decided to reorganize rural residence patterns and to use new housing programs to that end, they did not immediately inform the donors who were funding the programs. Nor did national authorities tell all of the agencies doing the construction about the new requirements to build only in government-designated sites. They left it to local officials to deliver the orders to some of them. When agencies which had been repairing or building houses outside imidugudu found their programs halted, they then carried the word back to the donors.[299]

The Dutch and the German representatives who had been discussing large contributions to housing programs in December 1996 were disconcerted to learn a month later that the government had initiated the imidugudu policy without even mentioning it to them. The U.S., which had $25 million earmarked for housing rehabilitation, found implementing agencies blocked in the field when they tried to rebuild houses.[300]

Donors were annoyed at not having been informed about the habitat policy. But beyond that many reacted negatively because they doubted that moving people into imidugudu would deliver the anticipated economic benefits. The representative of UNDP, for example, wrote that the dispersed habitat in Rwanda was not just a cultural preference but a rational strategy for survival given the current economic conditions.[301]

Donors raised other objections in terms of practical politics: they feared that dictating such a drastic change in living patterns from the top down could arouse popular animosity against the government and they worried that beginning such a major program without legislation could lead to legal complications.[302]

It seems that donors did not include possible human rights violations among their objections to rural reorganization even though they apparently understood very quickly that some rural-dwellers had been or might be forced to leave their homes against their will. In early February 1997, just weeks after the implementation of the policy began, the representative of the European Community Humanitarian Office, a funding agency of the European Union (E.U.), was so concerned about forcible relocation that he stated twice in a brief note that only programs of "voluntary settlement" could secure funding from the European Commission.[303] At a meeting a week later between representatives of embassies and humanitarian agencies, one participant reported that "in some parts of the country,

---

[299]Minutes, Meeting of diplomats regarding housing polcies, February 12, 1997.

[300]Human Rights Watch interview, Kigali, May 26, 2000; Minutes, meeting of diplomats regarding housing policies, February 12, 1997; Minutes, Meeting of diplomats regarding housing policies, February 21, 1997; Anonymous, "Imidugudu," pp. 6-8.

[301]Omar Bakhet, UNDP Resident Representative and U.N. Resident Coordinator to Ambassadors and Heads of U.N. agencies, January 23, 1997.

[302]Minutes, Meeting of diplomats regarding housing policies, February 12, 1997; Minutes, Meeting of diplomats regarding housing policies, February 21, 1997.

[303]European Community Humanitarian Office-Rwanda, Note for the File, Shelter funding criteria, February 5, 1997.

everybody is asked to pack and settle at new sites." Several participants doubted official assurances that coercion would not be used to force rural-dwellers to relocate.[304]

In early 1997 donors were already concerned enough about imidugudu to commission a study of the program which was completed in May 1997. In a generally negative assessment, the report summarized the experience of government-directed villagization efforts in other countries, all of which had failed. Drawing on the opinion of agricultural experts, it raised questions whether land consolidation would necessarily raise yields, particularly if cultivators lived at greater distances from their fields. It expressed concern too at the likelihood of crops or livestock being stolen from distant fields and at the probability that farmers would raise fewer head of livestock in the imidugudu. It deplored the waste of resources involved in destroying existing houses and abandoning near-by infrastructure like roads, wells, and latrines.[305]

The report went further to repeat the suspicions of some observers that the Rwandan government was seeking to undo that part of the Arusha Accords which effectively consigned Tutsi returnees to settlements in previously unoccupied—and largely undesirable—lands. These observers speculated that the government intended to move other rural-dwellers from their holdings and into imidugudu so that it could more easily redistribute desirable lands to the returnees.[306] The author of the study pointed out that such redistribution would violate both customary users' rights to the land and the guarantee given to Hutu refugees in the September 1996 ministerial order. The author also remarked that ". . .the choice of how to live and farm under the precondition that one does not harm the common interest is a fundamental human right."[307] He raised concerns that the government had decided a matter of "fundamental" interest to the 95 percent of the population who were cultivators without consulting them.[308] He concluded with some foresight that a program with so little popular backing could be executed only through the use of considerable coercion.[309] After extensive interviews with representatives of donors, multilateral agencies, and NGOs, the author of the study concluded, "Donors and implementing partners are unhappy with the plans. . . ."[310] Despite this general opposition to the policy, international actors mounted no coordinated, effective effort to deal with it.

In August 1997, the Ministry of Interior and Communal Development answered some of the criticisms formulated in the donor-sponsored report. It asserted that the cultural

---

[304]Minutes, Meeting of diplomats regarding housing policies, February 12, 1997.

[305]Anonymous, "Imidugudu," pp. 25-29.

[306]Anonymous, "Imidugudu," p. 6. As noted above, Human Rights Watch documented several cases of persons who moved to imidugudu after ceding all their land to returnees.

[307]Ibid., p. 27.

[308]Anonymous, "Imidugudu," draft working paper, pp. 11, 14.

[309]Anonymous, "Imidugudu," p. 25.

[310]Anonymous, "Imidugudu," p. 26.

context of Rwanda was different from that of other countries where government-directed villagization had failed and hence that their experience was not relevant. It affirmed once more that resettlement was to be voluntary, encouraged by economic incentives.[311]

Donors heard the official rhetoric of Kigali better than they heard complaints from the hills. Even representatives of donor countries or agencies responsible for contributing millions of dollars to housing programs apparently made little effort to inform themselves about life outside the capital and relied for information on subordinates and humanitarian workers who themselves learned to filter out information that did not conform to the official Rwandan description of the situation. One agricultural expert employed by an embassy said that Rwandan officials let him understand that continued public opposition to rural reorganization might result in a request for him to be withdrawn from Rwanda. He then fell silent on the topic.[312]

From mid-1997 through 1998, donors seem to have dropped criticism of rural reorganization while they poured large amounts of money into housing programs.[313] The U.S. was one of the few to end its bilateral aid to housing construction programs during this period. According to a U.S. AID employee, it did so because the programs were "messy," meaning troublesome to administer, not because they involved human rights abuses.[314] And, as noted below, the U.S. did continue to contribute through U.N. agencies.

When the Rwandan government moved more than 650,000 people into camps during the insurgency in the northwest, the donor community accepted the argument that security concerns made the displacement necessary and contributed $22 million to support the camps. But when the government found the situation sufficiently under control in late 1998 to begin disbanding the camps and moving the displaced into imidugudu, the donors began to balk at further contributions for housing programs. Perhaps because Rwanda that year launched its second war in the DRC—once more claiming the demands of security as justification—donors were increasingly sceptical that security in the ravaged northwest necessitated a complete reorganization of rural life. They also found it difficult to ignore the use of force and coercion in Ruhengeri and Gisenyi, prefectures where much attention had been focused because of the insurgency. That local officials oversaw the destruction of some houses while at the very same time the government was asking money to construct others contributed to disillusionment among the donors. In addition, some data seemed to indicate that rural reorganization might actually cut agricultural production instead of increasing it.

The E.U., whose representative was one of the first in 1997 to caution about the importance of resettlement being "voluntary," expressed the newly critical mood in July 1999. Its Council of Ministers urged "careful planning, prior impact studies and pilot

---

[311]Dorothea Hilhorst and Mathijs van Leeuwen, "Villagisation in Rwanda," Wageningen Disaster Studies, no. 2, 1999, Rural Development Sociology Group, Wageningen University, The Netherlands, p. 16.

[312]Human Rights Watch interview, Kigali, May 23, 2000.

[313]Human Rights Watch interviews, Kigali, May 23 and October 23, 2000.

[314]Human Rights Watch interview, Washington, by telephone, September 14, 2000.

projects in order to avoid villagisation that brings about human rights violations." Yet in the face of mounting evidence that "villagisation" was in fact resulting in human rights violations, the E.U. provided some $6 million that year to finance imidugudu.[315]

It is difficult to compute how much international aid was used to build houses in imidugudu. Assistance was sometimes funneled through budget lines that did not indicate exact use of the funds; aid from several donors sometimes paid for a single project; support for houses in imidugudu was not always distinguished from aid for houses built outside the sites. In addition, some bilateral aid was contributed through U.N. agencies.

Even with incomplete data, however, it is clear that international donors contributed tens of millions of dollars, most of which paid for construction in imidugudu.[316] UNHCR served as the major conduit of funds to building programs between 1996 and 1998 when it spent at least $30.7 million dollars to build houses or to provide materials to build houses. Of this amount, $20.6 million paid for houses in imidugudu and another $10 million paid for construction materials for houses, the majority of which were also built in imidugudu.[317] The Canadian Development Agency, the second most important donor after UNHCR, gave $16.3 million, at least $14.7 of which paid for houses built in imidugudu.[318] The Netherlands, one of the first to give, contributed $10 million, most of which went for housing, and the U.S. spent $6.1 million in the course of 1997 for housing. Japan was also a major donor. The European Union contributed some $6 million to build 6,000 houses in 1997 and another nearly $6 million in 1999. France built houses in five imidugudu for a cost of $1.2 million. Germany also paid for housing programs.[319] According to the Rwandan government, the Dutch, Japanese, Canadian and American governments were the largest donors through U.N. agencies.[320]

---

[315]United Nations. Economic and Social Council. Commission on Human Rights. "Report . . . by the Special Representative, Mr. Michel Moussalli," p. 32; Laurent and Bugnion, "External Evaluation of the UNHCR Shelter Program," p. 19.

[316]Houses built by the ECHO program averaged $1232 per unit between 1996 and 1998 and $794 per unit in 1999; those built by the French averaged $1,130 per unit; and those built by various Canadian-funded agencies cost some $1439, not including an expensive set of 100 houses built at a cost of $3900 by the city of Kigali. In some cases, donors provided only roofing materials, which ordinarily cost less than $200. Laurent and Bugnion, "External Evaluation of the UNHCR Shelter Program," pp. 19-21, 105-107.

[317]Laurent and Bugnion, "External Evaluation of the UNHCR Shelter Program," pp. 4, 19.

[318]Ibid., pp. 105-07.

[319]Ibid., pp. 18-21; Anonymous, "Imidugudu," pp. 6,8; Human Rights Watch interviews, Kigali, May 26, August 11 and 13, and by telephone, September 14, 2000.

[320]Government of Rwanda, "Thematic Consultation, pp. 8-9.

Difficult as it is to evaluate the total international contribution to housing programs, it is even more difficult to know how much of that money contributed to housing people who were homeless and how much contributed to housing people relocated against their will to imidugudu. And it is more difficult still to assess the extent to which the financial support of the housing programs betokened a political support which encouraged the Rwandan government to implement rural reorganization faster and more unconditionally than it might otherwise have done.

At the start international donors saw the imidugudu program as part of a long-term economic development effort and they discussed it in those terms. But as they realized that their criticism of rural reorganization created difficulties with the Rwandan government—which for many reasons they wanted to avoid—they accepted the official interpretation that imidugudu were necessary as an "emergency" response to an overwhelming housing crisis caused by the return of the refugees. By accepting this pretext, donors and representatives of international agencies relinquished the opportunity to examine rural reorganization in its appropriate context, as an undertaking for economic development. They failed to insist upon the usual requirements for planning, prior consultation with the target population, and enforcement of standards. And they failed to even consider, far less apply, international cautions against funding development projects that involve forced displacement. The U.N. Committee on Economic, Social and Cultural Rights stated in 1990, for example, that international agencies should "scrupulously" avoid involvement in projects which "involve large-scale evictions or displacement of persons without the provision of all appropriate protection and compensation."[321]

U.N. Agencies

U.N. agencies assisted enormously in implementing the resettlement program. Although aware of the abuses it entailed, they continued their support and failed to influence Rwandan authorities to end forcible displacement of rural-dwellers.

The most important international agency to participate in the imidugudu program was UNHCR which had been involved ever since the planning phase of the Arusha Accords. From its initial role as provider of emergency shelter for returnees it was drawn into the role of leading facilitator of the rural reorganization program. It provided about 80 percent of the funding channeled through U.N. agencies for housing construction.

At least one important UNHCR representative in Rwanda at the start of the imidugudu program disapproved of it and provided much of the critical analysis for the generally negative assessment sponsored by the donors, mentioned above. That document quoted a UNHCR representative as saying, "U.N. organizations do what governments want them to do in general, but they are fully sensitive to back-donors [i.e., the donors who support them]

---

[321] U.N. Committee on Economic, Social and Cultural Rights, General Comment No. 2 on the Right to Adequate Housing (Art. 11.1) Forced Evictions, 1990, paragraphs 6 and 8(d). See also Human Rights Watch, Written statement submitted to the Commission on Human Rights, E/CN.4/1996/NGO/41, 23 March 1996.

closing funding pipelines in rejection of governments [sic] policy."[322] The official continued that UNHCR favored a common strategy by donors and NGOs to deal with the imidugudu policy but stressed that UNDP—not UNHCR— should take the lead in creating this joint effort.

It is true that UNDP was charged with coordinating the efforts of all U.N. agencies and in this sense might have had responsibility for assuming leadership on this question, but it was UNHCR which had an explicit mandate to protect refugees, including those recently returned to their home country.

Given the situation in early 1997 when the habitat policy was launched, however, it is easy to suppose why UNHCR preferred not to lead opposition to the imidugudu program. It had been blamed for "feeding the genocidaires," the perpetrators of genocide, in the Zairean camps for two years and it had just endured several weeks of bitter conflict with the Rwandan government and its chief foreign backers, particularly the U.S., over the question of how many refugees were in the Zairean forests and how best to rescue them. Taking a firm stand against abuses in the resettlement program would have set UNHCR once more against the Rwandan government and might have entailed being forced out of the country.

Once UNHCR launched building programs, they grew rapidly and the critical voice inside the agency was apparently not heard again. Despite its intimate connection with the imidugudu program and the opportunity to witness abuses involved in its implementation, UNHCR never denounced such practices as the forcible displacement of rural-dwellers and the order to destroy houses.[323] Asked to comment on rural reorganization, one UNHCR staff member refused to make any assessment. "UNHCR is concerned only with shelter," she said, "not with government policy."[324]

UNDP, charged with long-term economic development programs, played a less important role in assisting resettlement, supplying perhaps 20 percent of the funding that came through U.N. agencies. According to one participant in UNDP meetings, abuses related to resettlement were never discussed within UNDP, even after the agency created a special unit for human rights issues.[325]

The two agencies differed in their approaches to resettlement programs: UNHCR focused on building houses as fast as possible, while UNDP favored more integrated projects involving infrastructure, services, and income-producing plans. The two agencies agreed to work together in 1997 and established the Joint Reintegration Programming Unit (JRPU) to facilitate this collaboration, yet they continued to have trouble coordinating their efforts, perhaps because they were similarly intent on using housing programs to maximize the

---

[322] Anonymous, "Imidugudu," p. 5.

[323] Human Rights Watch interview, Geneva, October 6, 2000.

[324] Human Rights Watch interview, Kigali, January 17, 2000.

[325] Human Rights Watch interview, Kigali, August 15, 2000.

amount of resources that came to their agencies.[326] Concern for human rights apparently dropped from view in this competition.

In late 1999 UNHCR sent a team of external evaluators to assess the imidugudu program.[327] Throughout the inquiry, local UNHCR agents stressed their role in providing "shelter," a term which suggested a short-term emergency response to the housing crisis provoked by the return of the refugees. But the evaluators concluded that UNHCR had done much more:

> In the case of the SP[shelter program], UNHCR has embarked in an operation that is much wider than just building shelter. It is directly responsible for participating in the implementation of a settlement policy, which will have long-term consequences altogether socially, economically and physically, and for which, up to now, sustainability has not been ensured.

Several paragraphs later, the report continues:

> In four years, the "imidugudu" policy has modified drastically the aspect of the rural landscape. The country is now covered with groups of tiny houses, all alike, whether in size, shape, or type of materials; and UNHCR has heavily contributed to this change by providing the materials or building 98,447 houses in 252 settlement sites and in scattered locations all over Rwanda.[328]

In contacts with the evaluators and others, UNHCR minimized its role in the imidugudu by stating that only some 25 percent of its resources went to building houses in the settlements. This refers to construction programs done under its direct supervision. The rest apparently paid for housing materials, primarily roofs, doors, and windows, that were distributed through local authorities. UNHCR says these materials built houses that were "scattered," implying that these houses were not in imidgudu. But the data, including

---

[326]CCA Working Paper, no. 3, p. 6; Laurent and Bugnion, "External Evaluation of the UNHCR Shelter Program," pp. 25-6; Hilhorst and van Leeuwen, "Villagisation in Rwanda," pp. 23-24. The World Food Program joined the JRPU in 1998 and representatives of other U.N. agencies collaborated with it occasionally.

[327]In order to assure maximum transparency, the investigators included a Rwandan government official and another Rwandan consultant to the Swiss embassy in their work team. Their presence in interviews may have considerably altered the quality and quantity of information provided by imidugudu residents.

[328]Laurent and Bugnion, "External Evaluation of the UNHCR Shelter Program," pp. xi-xiii.

interviews with imidugudu residents presented in the report, indicates that some—and probably the majority—of these materials were used to build houses in imidugudu.[329]

Although the evaluators criticized UNHCR involvement in the imidugudu program from several points of view, including the possibility that the settlements would not be economically sustainable, they failed to address the human rights abuses which had taken place during its implementation. They said only that the "absence of specific indicators" made it impossible for them to evaluate how well the program fulfilled the protection component of the UNHCR mandate, the component which includes questions of human rights.[330]

After reviewing their records, UNHCR officials in Geneva told a Human Rights Watch researcher that they could find no UNHCR report about or denunciation of human rights abuses in connection with the resettlement policy. One remarked, "We decided to keep our mouths shut and help those whom we could help." Another judged UNHCR conduct more severely, saying, "We were complicit. . . but so were all the U.N. agencies."[331]

The World Food Program provided food that was used to pay workers who built houses in many imidugudu. Although their agents frequently had contact with local people and witnessed the abuses to which they were subject, there is no indication that they protested against them or reported them systematically to their superiors.

The special representative for Rwanda of the U.N. Commission on Human Rights is charged with technical assistance in the field of human rights rather than with monitoring abuses. Nonetheless his opinion was sought—probably by donors—on issues related to the habitat policy. He visited three imidugudu after having heard allegations of the use of coercion to get rural-dwellers to move. After learning, as noted above, that twenty families in one umudugudu had been told to destroy their homes and relocate, he concluded that some coercion had occurred, often for reasons of security. He remarked that with security improving in the country, this justification would have declining relevance as a reason for obliging people to leave their homes. He added that the Guiding Principles on Internal Displacement require that persons displaced for security reasons be allowed to return home when the emergency is over.

But the special representative did not address the situation of persons coerced to move for other than security reasons—certainly the case for many—nor did he discuss their right to return to their former homes. He noted the reassurance given by a presidential adviser that "no Rwandans will be forced into villages against their will" and expressed the hope that this would become formal government policy. It is hard to understand such optimism, unless perhaps he had not known that government officials had first made the same guarantee in

---

[329]Laurent and Bugnion, "External Evaluation of the UNHCR Shelter Program," pp. xi, 4, 19, 63, 65. But some 13,000 of the 98,447 houses were repaired rather than built new and hence were likely not in imidugudu.

[330]Laurent and Bugnion, "External Evaluation of the UNHCR Shelter Program," p. x.

[331]Human Rights Watch interviews, Geneva, October 12, 13, and 26, 2000.

The Role of the International Community   83

1997 and had repeatedly violated it since. Aware of the importance of land to subsistence cultivators, the special representative encouraged greater debate on the habitat policy. But rather than clearly denouncing its abuses and insisting that those already displaced be permitted to return home, he recommended merely that the conditions of life be improved in existing settlements. He suggested that if services were provided before people were asked to move, rural-dwellers "would be clamouring for admission" to imidugudu.[332]

As noted below, the special representative endorsed the need for more funds in 2000 to build houses in imidugudu.

Nongovernmental Organizations

Of all the foreign parties involved in establishing imidugudu, the staff of NGOs were closest to the people suffering the abuses. By and large, they too kept silent about the hardships they witnessed. As resources flooded in to pay for the construction of houses, the Rwandan government informed many NGOs new to Rwanda—and new to housing construction—that they must start building programs. Rwandan authorities also set the terms under which the projects were to be carried out. Inexperienced NGOs quickly caved in to the pressure, many of them well aware that the government had expelled some two dozen NGOs more than a year before when they had failed to meet its expectations.

Some saw the well-funded housing contracts as a way to sustain their own presence in Rwanda and did not question the potentially negative effects of their work on some rural residents. Just as one UNHCR staff member shifted all responsibility for rural reorganization to the government, so one NGO employee put the burden on UNHCR as well as the government. He said: "If UNHCR offers you a job, you are happy to accept it. We are only invited [to do this work], the government and UNHCR set the policy."[333]

The staff of more scrupulous organizations worked harder to protect the interests of rural-dwellers. Those best established in Rwanda and most familiar with local politics sometimes managed to continue the programs they had begun, even if they did not conform to the imidugudu policy.[334]

In Kibungo, Umutara, and Kigali-rural, however, even the strongest NGOs found it difficult to implement their own policies and maintain their standards. The Lutheran World Federation (LWF), one of the best established NGOs in Rwanda, had staff who foresaw potential abuses in the imidugudu program. In March 1997, the head of its Kigali office informed other staff that: "People have the right to choose the manner in which they build and locate their houses, subject to the overriding concerns of a society as determined by its laws." Under the heading "policy," he noted:

> LWF will only assist with new villages in already settled areas when it is absolutely

---

[332] United Nations, Economic and Social Council, Commission on Human Rights, "Report . . . by the Special Representative, Mr. Michel Moussalli," pp. 32-33.

[333] Hilhorst and van Leeuwen, "Villagisation in Rwanda," p. 24.

[334] Human Rights Watch interview, by telephone, Washington, September 14, 2000.

clear that those being resettled:
Do not destroy the houses they are leaving, but vacate them for others
Are moving of their own free will
Will have a reasonable level of service in the sites to which they are moving.[335]

According to one senior staff member speaking in October 2000, "LWF still applies the principle" spelled out in 1997.[336]

The difficulty in upholding such principles emerge from the case of Ndego, an umudugudu in Kibungo where LWF assisted in building the houses. Land at the new site is infertile and dry and the new settlement lies in the former game park, distant from other population centers. According to the UNHCR evaluation report, some 166 families from the neighboring commune of Nyarubuye were forced to come to the umudugudu against their will, leaving behind lands that were then turned over to a single person, reportedly a military officer. When asked about the case, the senior LWF staff member said the agency was responsible only for building the houses, not for choosing who would occupy them. She added that when some 400 to 500 families returned from Tanzania in 1997, authorities declared that the returnees could not go back to their homes because the region was insecure and that they had to settle instead in the umudugudu. The security threat is long since finished, but the families remain in the settlement site while the land around their former homes is used to pasture cattle. As a result of the visit of the UNHCR evaluation team, this case was reported to the authorities and has received some attention which might help remedy this abuse.[337]

---

[335] John Cosgrave to Project Coordinators, Lutheran World Federation, March 4, 1997.

[336] Human Rights Watch interview by telephone, Geneva, October 13, 2000.

[337] Ibid; Laurent and Bugnion, "External Evaluation of the UNHCR Shelter Program," pp. 44, 96.

XVI. DIALOGUE WITH THE RWANDAN GOVERNMENT

When foreign criticism of rural reorganization mounted and international assistance for housing construction correspondingly declined in late 1998 and 1999, Rwandan officials launched a new initiative to obtain international support for the program. In July 1999, the Ministry of Lands, Human Resettlement and Environmental Protection reaffirmed the rural reorganization policy, saying "Imidugudu will [be] the only recommended and promoted form of settlement in rural areas. The ultimate objective of the Government is to enable the *entire* rural population to live in the grouped settlements."[338] Although unyielding on the policy itself, most officials, including President Kagame, conceded that there had been problems with its implementation. Kagame told donors in July 1999, "There have been a few setbacks during the implementation phase, which varied with local leadership. However, the experience has generally been positive and we shall correct the deficiencies as we move along."[339] For its part, the ministry claimed that shortcomings in implementation had resulted from "the vast number of people in need of urgent shelter; the consequent pressure on local authorities; the 'large number of NGOs involved in the exercise;' and the limited coordination capacity of the Government."

The ministry also promised that a "participatory" approach would characterize implementation of the policy in the future, seeming to suggest that coercion would not be used. And, in fact, residents in the northwest indicated that in several cases local authorities did not follow through with planned announcements of impending relocations during 2000. In August 2000, one person from Ruhengeri commented, "At one point, the burgomaster and the prefect said just wait, we will destroy your houses and put you in sheeting. Now the prefect says that it is not necessary to destroy houses. Give people time to build as they have the means. This is a big relief for us."[340]

In the second half of 1999 and during 2000, authorities also made efforts to improve the conditions in those imidugudu where residents lived in the worst squalor. The national government promised to provide some 20 million Rwandan francs or $50,000 for roofing and the prefects of Ruhengeri and Gisenyi both said they were encouraging local enterprises which could produce roofing materials at low cost for local people.[341] Conditions in the large umudugudu in Kinigi, one of the worst in the northwest, benefitted from new resources and official attention after President Kagame visited and promised improvements in August 2000. The government sought to encourage visits by foreign tourists to the gorilla preserve in the volcanoes just north of Kinigi and visitors must drive through this commune to enter the park; this, too, may have played a part in the decision to improve conditions there. At the end of 2000, visitors no longer saw blindés but rather wood-framed houses in Kinigi. Most

---

[338] CCA Working Paper, no. 3, p. 7. Emphasis in the original.

[339] Ibid.

[340] Human Rights Watch interview, Kigali, August 5, 2000.

[341] Human Rights Watch interviews, Gisenyi, January 14, 2000 and Ruhengeri, February 25, 2000.

houses appeared smaller than those found in other imidugudu and the quality of construction of the walls varied considerably, with some being made of leaves, others mud, others plastic sheeting, or pieces of metal. Some of these houses had metal roofs which were distributed among residents by lottery since there were not enough for everyone. At the time of one visit in late December, local people were breaking rocks into gravel along the roads. They said the gravel would be used to make concrete for foundations for the houses. Outside the umudugudu, there were no houses at all, although the concrete or stone foundations of former homes were still visible, some with vegetation sprouting through them.[342]

In efforts to push the international community to renewed generosity, Rwandan authorities continued to stress the overwhelming scale of the housing emergency, which, they said, was not quite finished. They sometimes exaggerated the extent of the crisis by totaling the numbers of all returnees—"old" and "new"— to arrive at a total of 2,670,000[343] and by failing to distinguish between returnees, mostly Tutsi, who came from the outside with nothing and the far-larger number of Hutu returnees who had homes they could reoccupy, even if they required repairs. Having depicted the overwhelming nature of the crisis, officials then insisted that they had had no choice but to impose the resettlement policy, particularly in view of the need for reconciliation and promoting social harmony. In one such presentation to a donors' meeting in London, then Vice-President Kagame said, "In a society attempting to heal from the genocide the potential for exacerbating tension and conflict due to limited land resources cannot be underestimated. In many instances there was no alternative where 4 million (sic) people had to be settled."[344]

Government officials often tried to make international actors feel at least indirectly responsible for the problems linked to the imidugudu. They implied that many of the deficiencies resulted from the dwindling of international aid and could be remedied by increasing that aid. One senior official even suggested that the reduction in foreign aid demonstrated partiality to the Hutu—that donors became sufficiently concerned about problems of implementation to cut assistance only after the imidugudu program touched people of the northwest.[345]

Skillful in playing upon foreigners' sense of guilt about their conduct in Rwanda, government officials also called upon other possible arguments to persuade international actors to support the imidugudu plan. In one case, a bishop—perhaps with official encouragement—tried to persuade a foreign ambassador in Kigali that women benefitted particularly from the establishment of imidugudu: he asserted that husbands beat their wives less often in the settlements because they feared embarrassment if neighbors were to hear the

---

[342] Human Rights Watch, field notes, December 28, 2000.

[343] From 1994 through 1999. Government of Rwanda, "Thematic Consultation, p. 2.

[344] CCA Working Paper, no. 3, p. 8.

[345] Human Rights Watch interview, Kigali, October 23, 2000.

noise of the beating. Given that women were among those to suffer most from forced relocation, this claim of benefit to women seemed especially cynical.[346]

To dispel skepticism resulting from earlier "lack of transparency"[347] about the intended objectives of the resettlement program, government officials in late 1999 began a dialogue with representatives of donors, U.N. agencies, and NGOs. They worked through the steering committee of the JRPU, the coordination unit for U.N. agencies mentioned above, to which they submitted a report about imidugudu in early December 1999.

This report finally spurred international interluctors to confront the continuing confusion between housing for the homeless and the rural reorganization program. In a note prepared by the Belgian, British, Canadian, French, German, Italian, Swedish, Swiss and Netherlands embassies and cooperation missions, they asked whether dialogue with the government was "meant 'to deal with the issue of the lack of shelter' or rather the "current practice" of 'resettlement' (moving people that already have shelter). . . ." They stated further:

> Shelter for the homeless, rehabilitating damaged shelter and relocating people who have shelter are not necessarily contradictory policies. However, they are different and must be clearly distinguished, especially as the latter implies abandoning existing shelter. . . .[348]

The donors asked for "a clear chronology of relevant legislation" and said that "designing a policy without a clear legal framework seems rather useless." They called for coherent statistics and pointed out the discrepancies in the report between the estimation that some 370,000 persons needed homes—which would mean some 74,000 homes—and the statement that some 300,000 homes were needed. And they insisted that the government's new "strategy" of a "participatory approach" needed further elaboration. "The mere statement about 'involving the population at all levels of the process' is extremely meagre, . . ." they said. They added, "The fact that the population will be forced to change their traditional way of living should equally not be disregarded."[349].

Other international interlocutors also raised the need for more detailed information the proposed "participatory" approach to changing rural life. A memo from UNDP talked about the importance of a "consensual" solution to resettlement.[350] Similarly, the international

---

[346] Human Rights Watch interview, Kigali, April 10, 1999.

[347] CCA Working Paper, no. 3, p. 7.

[348] Discussion Note on the Report to the Steering Committee Meeting on Resettlement (2 December 1999) addressed to Ms. Patricia Hajabakiga, Secretary General, Ministry of Land, Human Resettlement and Environmental Protection, 24 December 1999.

[349] Ibid.

[350] UNDP Memo, "Common UNDP Position on Assistance in the context of the Imidugudu Policy" [December, 1999].

NGO forum commented that the new government rhetoric about popular involvement was not backed by concrete measures. It asked, "Will participation be more than 'sensitisation' at the planning stage, more than 'agreeing' at site identification stage, more than making bricks at the implementation stage?"[351]

The official charged with responding to these criticisms simply asserted that "The GoR arrived at this decision [to implement the habitat policy] as a result of broad consultations at all levels."[352] This claim misrepresented the history of the policy, as detailed above.

After months of dialogue, Rwandan authorities in July 2000 formulated a request for $400 million, about three times the total national budget for the fiscal year 2000, to provide housing for an estimated 370,000 households. This number represented an increase of 120,000 over the number estimated to need housing in 1997 despite the construction of more than 100,000 houses in the interim. The request did not explain this puzzling increase in need.[353]

The appeal for funds simply stressed that the housing emergency continued and that the money was needed for the truly vulnerable persons living in miserable conditions. Authorities played again on the key words that proved so successful in the past, claiming that the program promoted reconciliation and security. The objectives for which the habitat policy was originally developed—the rationalization of land use and the promotion of economic development—were mentioned last as reasons for the settlement policy.[354]

As in the previous July, the government claimed that the problems involved in implementing the imidugudu program resulted from the urgency of the crisis, the number of NGOs building the houses, and the lack of coordination by and with the government. But in this bid for renewed support, it acknowledged the problems in greater the detail. It said that locating imidugudu on fertile, flat land forced residents to cultivate less fertile slopes, "risking low yields and environmental degradation." It cited construction of houses which were "too small, too close together, and lacked privacy." It said also that local people "were not generally involved in site selection, house design, plot size decision making or other aspects of planning and implementing the resettlement policy. The result was a lack of ownership on the part of the people who are expected to live in the *imidugudu*." It mentioned "great disparities of access to social services for people living in *imidugudu*," particularly in access to clean water. Among other criticisms, it included the "lack of income-generating activities and market access" and "social issues including the lack of social cohesion and

---

[351]"Comments from the NGO Thematic Group on Settlement and Land Issues on the Report of the Thematic Consultation on Resettlement," enclosed in letter from the NGO Thematic Group on settlement and villagisation to Mrs. Patricia Hajabakiga, Secretary General, Ministry of Land, Human Resettlement and Environmental Protection, Kigali, 10/01/2000.

[352]Patricia Hajabakiga to Ms. Jeannette Seppen, First Secretary, Embassy of the Netherlands, Kigali, 11/1/2000, no. 013/16.02, with copies to nine other recipients.

[353]Government of Rwanda, "Thematic Consultation, pp. 1, 23.

[354]CCA Working Paper, no. 3, pp. 8-9.

risks of 'ghettoization,'" apparently a reference to the monoethnic nature of most imidugudu.[355]

In increasingly critical correspondence with the Rwandan authorities in late 1999 and 2000, foreign funders apparently did not raise directly the use of coercion or force in relocating rural residents, but they reportedly did talk about this issue in discussions with officials. Rwandan authorities responded that local officials had never been instructed to use force and that those who had done so had acted on their own initiative. They provided no explanation about why these cases were so numerous, why they happened more frequently in some prefectures than in others, or why national officials had not intervened to end the abuses. According to one participant in these discussions, the question was simply dropped when it became clear that donors and Rwandan authorities could not reach consensus on it.[356] Still the funding request seemed to take account of this concern. It stated:

> At the same time, it is important to underscore that resettlement in the Rwandan context involves providing habitat for people who do not currently have suitable accommodation. It does not involve removing people from suitable homes which they legally occupy.[357]

The government promised also that implementation would involve "broad consultations at all levels." It continued:

> Guidelines on the implementation of the policy will be made available to all stakeholders, particularly those at the grassroots level. These will include [the]legal context of the programme regarding land, rights of *imidugudu* inhabitants and a complaints procedure.[358]

By October 2000 the government had not defined the "rights" of imidugudu residents, nor did important local officials—at least in Kibungo prefecture—want others to do so. Representatives of a human rights association organized training seminars in September and October for elected officials at the cell and sector level in Kibungo. According to national authorities, these officials at the grassroots level were to play a key part in assuring a "participatory" approach to implementing the habitat policy. When the human rights trainers explained guarantees of property and housing rights in international and Rwandan law, members of the audience at several sessions raised concerns about measures to force people into imidugudu and to appropriate their land. Prefectural officials present at the meetings disapproved of such questions and the prefect of Kibungo asked the trainers to give less

---

[355] Government of Rwanda, "Thematic Consultation, pp. 9-11.

[356] Human Rights Watch interviews, Kigali, July 13, August 15, 2000.

[357] Government of Rwanda, "Thematic Consultation," p. 1.

[358] Government of Rwanda, "Thematic Consultation," p. 25.

attention to property rights in future presentations.[359] In another case, the semi-official newspaper *Imvaho Nshya* criticized the minister for internal security and a parliamentary deputy for "sowing confusion" in alleged secret meetings organized in their prefecture of origin, Cyangugu. According to the journalist, the willingness of people to share their lands diminished as a result of these meetings, which were also supposedly linked to upcoming elections.[360]

At the end of 2000, government authorities seemed to be using persuasion more than coercion to persuade rural dwellers to relocate. They advertised the benefits of living grouped together on the radio and they brought delegations from other prefectures to Kibungo to visit imidugudu.[361]

But in some areas, including Cyangugu prefecture, officials continued to move people against their will into imidugudu. Authorities also initiated a new round of sharing the land in the prefecture of Gikongoro where the policy had not been in effect and where relatively few returnees had settled. Officials spurred landholders in two sectors of Karama commune to share their property with returnees who arrived in Gikongoro in late 2000 after having spent several years in Kigali or elsewhere in Rwanda. Like several of the cases mentioned above, some of those called upon to cede their land to returnees then decided to move to imidugudu, apparently because they had no more land left or too little left to provide for their subsistence.[362]

---

[359]Human Rights Watch interviews, Kigali, October 23 and 31, 2000.

[360]Frank Ndamage, "Rwaka and Nsabimana Sow Confusion in Cyangugu Prefecture," *Imvaho Nshya*, no. 1365, December 4-10, 2000.

[361]Radio Rwanda, evening news, November 25 and December 11, 2000.

[362]Radio Rwanda, Evening News, November 2, 2000.

XVII. CONCLUSION

Donors have been largely unmoved by Rwandan government appeals for aid to build more imidugudu and resistant to the suggestion that the current misery of the homeless results from an untimely end to previous international assistance. In November 2000, however, the Special Representative for Rwanda of the U.N. Commission on Human Rights told the General Assembly that 350,000 displaced persons in Rwanda lived "in very precarious conditions under plastic sheeting" and needed assistance. He did not explain the figure, which approximated the 370,000 cited by the Rwandan government, nor did he elaborate on how the affected persons had been displaced, a point of major importance[363]

Hundreds of thousands of persons suffer on the hills of Rwanda but insufficient international aid is only a tangential and not a fundamental cause of their misery. They suffer from the anguish and disruption of genocide and war, from poverty, hunger, disease, and despair. Tens of thousands of them suffer also from the changes caused by the imposition of the rural resettlement policy: the forced displacement from their homes, the waste of resources entailed by the destruction of houses, the reduction in productivity which has resulted from having to live far from their fields, and the loss of land given over to imidugudu. Many suffer also from having been obliged to "share" their land with or "return" it to those who have come back to Rwanda after a generation in exile.

The imidugudu program, generally understood by international actors to address the housing crisis, encapsulated also an effort to deal with the broader issues of economic development. Whether rural reorganization offers an effective solution to this major problem is debatable. What is not debatable is that the implementation of this program resulted in human rights abuses for tens of thousands of Rwandans.

With support for further imidugudu not forthcoming, the Rwandan government and the donors have moved from discussing resettlement to considering draft proposals on the larger issue of land-holding. Both in designing and in implementing a land policy, the Rwandan government should respect basic human rights, including the rights to choice of residence, to secure enjoyment of one's home, and to property. In those complex cases where there are competing rights, such as the conflicting claims to property, it must at least establish an equitable procedure for resolving these disputes and appropriate remedies for those who believe their rights have been abused. Donors and international agencies called upon to assist programs to house Rwandans or to change the system of land tenure must ensure that the policies they support not render homeless those now secure in their houses and lands nor otherwise violate the rights of Rwandans.

---

[363]United Nations, 55th Session of the General Assembly, (Third Committee), Statement of the Special Representative for Rwanda of the United Nations Commission on Human Rights, Mr. Michel Moussalli, November 1, 2000.